"Veronica Chambers does the kind of truth-telling about becoming an artist and a woman that made me kiss the pages of this book!"

—Veronica Webb,
contributing editor,
Interview magazine

The Joy of
Doing Things
Badly

The Joy of Doing Things Badly

A Girl's Guide to

Love, Life, and

Foolish Bravery

Veronica Chambers

BROADWAY BOOKS

New York

BROADWAY

Visit our Web site at www.broadwaybooks.com

"One Art" from THE COMPLETE POEMS: 1927–1979 by Elizabeth Bishop. Copyright © 1979, 1983 by Alice Helen Methfessel. Reprinted by permission of Farrar, Straus and Giroux, LLC.

This work is based on an article that first appeared in O, The Oprah Magazine.

Book design by Mauna Eichner
Illustrated by Sujean Rim

Library of Congress Cataloging-in-Publication Data
Chambers, Veronica.
    The joy of doing things badly : a girl's guide to love, life, and foolish bravery / Veronica Chambers.—1st ed.
        p.   cm.
    1. Women—Psychology. 2. Women—Conduct of life. 3. Self-doubt.
4. Self-confidence. I. Title.
HQ1206.C42 2006
305.242'20973—dc22   2005043519

ISBN-13: 978-0-385-51212-1
ISBN-10: 0-385-51212-0

PRINTED IN THE UNITED STATES OF AMERICA

10 9 8 7 6 5 4 3 2 1

First Edition

For Jason

Whose Laughter Is Joy

Acknowledgments

Thank you, first and foremost, to Janet Hill, editor extraordinaire and all around swell gal. Thanks as well to her assistant, Tracy Jacobs. Dawn Raffel, who assigned me the original "Joy" essay—*je vous remercie*. Jen De La Fuente along with Jerry and Mary Clampet read early drafts, and Jason read every draft. My nieces and nephews fill me with unending joy. My brother, Malcolm X Chambers, is good for jokes, board games, and sweet voice-mail messages from my nephew wishing me good night. *Grazie* to my manager, Angela Kyle, who consistently finds me work that I can do with joy. My aunt, Diana Richards, is a joy beacon.

A big, joyful thanks to Sujean Rim for her amazing illustrations; I feel lucky to have gotten to know her.

A big, swervilicious shout-out to the lovely Kris Hackel for being my partner in crime at Yoga Booty Ballet and Bhangra Bollywood dance class. Fellowships enable me to keep reaching toward the writing that I want to do. I can count on a wonderful posse of mentors and friends for recommendations: I am especially thankful to John Leland, Carol Rigolot, Chang-Rae Lee, David Gates, and Bernie Rodgers, who have given me more than I could ever express.

I am grateful for new friends: the Boys—Dario and Misja; the Gourmands—Andrew and Diana; and for old friends—especially Louise Hillman, Andrea Polans, and Caroline Kim. One of my big joys is the time I've spent in Japan: *domo* to Mina, Kazuko, Ritsuka, and DJ Naomi. I would like to thank Haruki, Jun, and Kazu, but Wakkaterutemo! Rancho La Puerta is a haven, as is One and Only Palmilla and the wonderful Wheatleigh Hotel. Vivianne Njoku does a bang-up job editing the "Joy of Doing Things Badly" newsletter. Send her an e-mail at joyofdoingthingsbadly@yahoo.com. You can reach me at www.veronicachambers.com.

Contents

The Joy of
Doing Things
Badly

Introduction: The Joy of Doing Things Badly

L AST SUMMER, MY HUSBAND, JASON, AND I WENT TO see my friend's daughter perform in her school play. The production was called *Thirteen Dancing Princesses*. We were early, so we gathered with my friend and her family in the courtyard of the school. Jason asked what the play was about. Gretchen told him, "There are thirteen teenage girls in it. Basically, there is a lot of crying and costume changes." Jason replied, "Sounds a lot like our house." Which made everyone laugh but also has the virtue of being the truth.

That said, if I didn't have a wealth of ugly habits, shortcomings, and failures, I wouldn't be so well qualified to write a book called *The Joy of Doing Things Badly.* Truly I say unto you, I'd have to destroy a rain forest to commit to paper my multiple, albeit pedestrian, flaws. At times, I have thought that it is a mighty cruel joke that God could bestow on me such a yearning for perfection—the loud and resounding voice within that Sue Bender calls "the judge"—alongside so little ability to reach my myriad and lofty goals. When I was a child, I thought "Humpty Dumpty" was just a story, like "Cinderella" or "The Three Little Bears." I did not know that it was a parable of fear and failure and loss. What this book is about, at the very heart of it, is how, time after time, with no help from all the king's horses and all the king's men, you *can* put yourself back together again.

Throughout my life, my willingness to fall flat on my face has been my most marked characteristic. Never having had money, I have always been willing to spend the one thing that I have in hefty supply: time. In the ninth grade, I learned that one boarding school scholarship would be awarded to an "underprivileged student" at my school. I spent months on the application, dreaming myself into the school uniform and onto the school's campus. In the end, I didn't get in.

In tenth grade, a guidance counselor encouraged me to apply to be the school's nominee for a year-long exchange program with a high school in Germany. I got the school nomination; but again, I didn't get the scholarship. By then, however, I had a taste for applications, and applying for things became the one thing that I was actually good at. I won a one-week scholarship to a girls' leadership program at Chestnut Hill College in Pennsylvania. I won a two-week scholarship to a teen journalism program in New Jersey. At sixteen, I was accepted to Simon's Rock College, a college for kids who wanted to go to college early. And when I was eighteen, I won the thing that would forever shape my life: an internship at a magazine called *Sassy*.

The thing about that particular internship is that it came fresh on the heels of what felt like another failure. A friend of mine had interned at *YM* magazine. She encouraged me to apply to *Seventeen* magazine, the fabled land of Sylvia Plath and Brooke Shields and Phoebe Cates. My friend Susan encouraged me to apply for an internship at the magazine as well. I was promptly turned down. But I refused to be discouraged. I got out a copy of the Manhattan Yellow Pages and I called every publication in the "magazine" section starting with *A*. I did not know that "Hello, do you have any internships?" was not the way to get ahead in the publishing business. For more than four hours, I was hung up on, transferred, and then hung up on again; I was told no in almost every conceivable fashion. Then I got to *S* and called up a magazine called *Sassy*, which just happened to be a new magazine for teenage girls. I was transferred to the managing editor, who very kindly invited me to send her a letter and my résumé and then invited me in for a meeting.

My first failure helped me: An internship at *Sassy*, led to an internship at *Seventeen*, which led to internships at *Essence* and *Life*. By the time I was twenty-one, I had an assortment of short clippings with my very own byline, and I began to believe that I was really and truly a writer. I'll never forget being invited to a fancy cocktail party by a powerful editor at a magazine where I worked. At this party, I was buttonholed by an older man, a surgeon of some renown in his field who had published some short stories to great acclaim. He asked me what I wanted to do, now that I had graduated and was beginning my literary career. I told him that I wanted to write a book. His laugh was loud and hearty. "Of course, you do," he said, and it seemed to me that "of course" had a dozen syllables in his mouth, each one more mocking than the last. "But you won't write anything of importance until you're thirty." I asked him what I was supposed to do in the nine years between twenty-one and thirty. He shrugged. This in itself turned out to be a very powerful lesson: There is no shortage of people who will tell you what you *can't* do, but these same people don't always have a lot of encouraging advice about what you *should* be doing. It's as if filling you with trepidation is their sole purpose in life.

A year later, when I was twenty-two, I was invited by the filmmaker John Singleton to write a "making of" movie book for his second film, *Poetic Justice.* When John called me, I thought of my conversation with the naysaying surgeon, and I wondered what he might have me do. Should I have told John Singleton, the youngest person ever to be nominated for a Best Director Academy Award (he was twenty-five at the time), "I'm only twenty-two, call me in eight years when I am thirty?" I didn't think so. What I did, what I always do, is give it my very best shot. I once heard an actor say that whenever you are asked in the course of an audition if there's something you can do, say yes: yes, you can juggle knives, roller skate backward, build a boat with your bare hands. Say yes because there's a chance you'll get the job, and then you'll have the time to learn. So that's what I did when John asked me to write the *Poetic Justice* book. I moved to Los Angeles where I did not know a soul. I took three buses to get to the movie studio where the film was being shot while I studied diligently for my driver's license. During that first month, when I spent hours on the bus, I often thought, "If only the people on this bus knew that I was on my way to a movie set with Janet Jackson and Tupac Shakur." But a girl's gotta do what a girl's gotta do. I took the bus to the set until I passed my driving test.

I did not own a computer so I wrote the book, my first book, on a secondhand electric typewriter. This, as you might imagine, took forever. Imagine the combination: A minuscule amount of talent, the attention span of a fruit fly (ask my friends, I do not exaggerate), and a typewriter that was so old it predated the correction ribbon. This meant that I wrote a draft of the chapter, corrected it by hand, then very carefully typed it in. When I was done with the book, I went immediately to the copy shop and made six copies, for fear that I would lose the original. This, in 1992, when the rest of the world (or so it seemed) was tooling along happily on fast, efficient PCs.

Sometimes, when I think back on that *Poetic Justice* book, I want to cringe. I could write that book a million times better today, but the fact is that the opportunity to write the book did not come to me when I was overqualified for the role. It came to me when I had to reach for it. And while my writing skills might be better today, I could not write that book today because John would not be making his sophomore film today; Janet Jackson would not be starring in her first feature film today; and Tupac Shakur, Janet's co-star in the film, is not alive today. I look back at that time, and I know that the joy of writing that book was not in my genius prose, but simply in being there: up front and counted for, when life came a-calling.

I am as ungifted in my play as I am in my work. I do not see my friend Liba as much as I would like. We have lived in the same city for over a year and between our new marriages and her new baby and our crazy jobs, we have gotten together less than a half a dozen times. But time with her is always inspirational. Liba, who is a visual artist and movie production designer, once gave me a set of watercolors and paper, which sat on the shelf for years because I'd never learned to draw, let alone paint, anything more than a smiley face. I couldn't waste that lovely paper on smiley faces. Besides—and this was always a clincher—who would I show my artwork to? I don't think I'm alone in my elementary-school affinity for show-and-tell. Why learn a piece of music unless it's to be performed? Why knit a sweater unless it's to be given to a loved one? We think everything we do has to be up to snuff, and we forget that the pure, uncensored joy of living in our own skin comes when we are not attached, 24/7, to either our fans or our critics. We can paint just for ourselves. We can belt out torch songs in an empty office when everyone else has gone home, and we can tango across the living room solo. No one's going to stop us from baking soufflés that fall and eating them in the privacy of our own kitchens. Trust me on this one: Chocolate doesn't have to be beautiful to taste really, really good.

Sometimes ethnic stereotypes make our shortfalls all the more painful. My posse of friends is brimming with black girls who can't play basketball, Latinas who don't speak Spanish well, and Asians who can't do math. "Black girls are supposed to be able to dance!" moans my friend Ali, who awkwardly muddled through our hip-hop adolescence and its complicated dances. These days, Ali is more comfortable with how her body moves, whatever people might say or think. She keeps on grooving even when she reaches the inevitable moment on the dance floor when, she says, "I realize I have lost the beat with no clue as to where to find it." When Liu Xiang won the 110-meter high hurdles at the 2004 Olympics in Athens, he gained the nickname "The Yellow Bullet," a nickname that he embraced. "It is unbelievable—a Chinese, an Asian, has won this event." It has long been accepted in the world of track and field, that Asians do not run as fast as their American, African, and European counterparts. "It is a proud moment," Mr. Liu told reporters, "not only for China, but for Asia and for all people who share the same yellow color." He is the first Chinese person to win a sprinting event in modern Olympic history.

The fear of doing something badly can affect more than just sports and entertainment. My friend Jenny remembers that before she decided to have a child, she was deeply afraid of being a bad mother. Off-key sonatas will be forgotten, but the mistakes we make with our children threaten to haunt us our entire lives. It was only when she got comfortable with the idea that she would certainly do many things wrong as a mother that she was able to go ahead and get pregnant. "The thing about doing things badly is that if you keep doing them, sometimes you get better," she says, as we walk down a tree-lined street toward the pizza parlor, her daughter speeding happily on Rollerblades ahead of us.

I've learned that it's a blessing when you can take something you once weighted down with shame and turn it into a pleasure. There's an art to doing things badly, especially in a society that puts so much emphasis on beauty, perfection, and achievement. Most of us talk ourselves out of doing anything we're not good at. Maybe we don't admit that our egos drive us to put forth only our brightest and best selves. We are, after all, so busy. Who has time for something we fully expect to be miserable at?

The "Birthday Passions" is what I call them. For my birthday, every year, I've decided to not to buy myself something but to indulge in something I never expect to master. The first Birthday Passion was a simple gift: Jane

Austen Thursdays. Every Thursday afternoon, I gave myself one hour to read Jane Austen. I started with her first
novel and my plan was to work my way through all six of
them. The beauty of it was that I had to read Austen only
for that hour. There was no rushing to finish the book for
a book club or a class. Whether I read ten pages or a hundred pages of Austen on a Thursday afternoon, it was good
enough. In fact, it was wonderful. I had read *Pride and Prejudice* in college but hadn't had much appreciation for it,
largely I think because I was taking six courses at the time
and working three campus jobs. Careening through
Austen at three o'clock in the morning did little to trans-
port me to the drawing rooms and country estates in
which her characters pondered the correlation between
virtue and wealth.

When I was in my twenties, Jane Austen enjoyed a re-
vival in cinema. While everyone always says that the
movies are never as good as the books, it was the movies
that brought me back to Jane. *Mansfield Park;* Gwyneth Paltrow in *Emma;* and my all time favorite, Emma Thompson's *Sense and Sensibility.* I saw the latter in the theater seven
times. When at a professional luncheon some years later I
had the chance to meet the film's producer, Lindsay Doran, I think I frightened her, just a little bit, with my obsession with the film. But it's she I have to thank for the
Birthday Passions. It was through reading her introduc-

tion to the published version of the screenplay that I learned how she had spent a dreary semester abroad in London, curled up in a library reading Austen, in the order the books were written, from the first book to the last. It sounded like heaven and, as I discovered when I undertook the task, it *was*.

Duplicating Doran's journey through Austen became a great pleasure: one hour a week, doing exactly as I pleased. There are so many things I want to incorporate into my daily routine: meditation and yoga and a nightly stroll after dinner. I want to write letters, not e-mails. I want to get up early and go to the wholesale flower market downtown instead of buying overpriced roses that wilt in two days at the local florist. I want fruits and vegetables from the farmers' market, and I want to feel the breeze in my hair as I ride my bicycle to that market. But sometimes, all the time really, these things feel out of reach. I do yoga one week and then promptly lose my Zen when I realize that I am, again, out of toilet paper and laundry detergent. I wake up and do a morning meditation; but the minute I sit, cross-legged, I can't help but think that if I have only an hour to spare before I have to get to work, I really need to be dragging my lard butt to a gym. The beauty of the Birthday Passions, beginning with the dive into Austen, is that all I had to do was show up for an hour each week. One goal instead of twenty; one new, fresh, and interesting resolution instead of the same old chorus of shoulda, coulda, woulda.

As the weeks went on, I made my Jane Austen Thursdays cozier. I brewed a pot of tea. I heated up a scone. I treated myself to the loveliest jam that I could find. And for one hour a week, sometimes two, sometimes three if time permitted, I nestled under a wool throw and allowed myself to be transported to the world of *Pride and Prejudice*, *Sense and Sensibility*, and *Mansfield Park*.

I started in September, but by the time December came, I was so busy that I never got back to my Thursdays. My initial instinct was to be frustrated: Why was my life so busy that I could not finish six novels in a year's time? Instead, I chose to be happy for what I was able to do. For three heavenly months, I reveled in this time. I'll get to those other three novels, eventually. And I dream of the day when I can carve out the time to devote one afternoon a week to exploring other authors that I love: Margaret Atwood Mondays, Toni Morrison Tuesdays.

When I was a child, my mother always used a certain Spanish expression: "*Las cosas se hacen bien o no se hacen*" ("Do things well or not at all"). I understand the logic of this, but in the end, this has not been a philosophy I choose to live by. The joy of doing things badly means that, in the process of leaving things undone, there is always something left to do. Someday I will learn how to drive a stick shift—or not. At some point in the future, probably when I retire, I will meditate twice a day. I like this image of myself, silver-haired and calm. If I were a picture of peace now, in the midst of my go-go thirties, perhaps it would be fortune delivered too soon. Maybe like a child star, I would find that too much success early on is bound to lead to bad things. Someday, I will learn how to swim. In the meantime, I drive an automatic and meditate once a week, and, as embarrassed as I am to admit it, I have been known to wrestle with small children in the shallow end of the pool for the last remaining noodle or arm floatie thingee, or whatever it is I need to be confident that I won't drown.

I have a friend who mocks me for not keeping up with popular culture. "I can't believe you haven't seen [Insert name of popular/award-winning/ground-breaking film here]." "I can't believe you haven't read [Insert name of popular/award-winning/ground-breaking book here]." She doesn't mean to mock me. She means to educate me, to make sure that I am keeping up on the latest trends. What I've learned is that if you live long enough, then the things you want most in life will wait for you. I recently read a book that I have been carrying from apartment to apartment for fourteen years: *Bicycle Days* by John Burnham Schwartz. When I first bought the book, I was intrigued by the cover. I did not know then that I would eventually, like the protagonist in the novel, travel and live in Japan. Reading the novel so many years later was all the sweeter because I knew the terrain of the book in a way that I could not have possibly known it when I was younger.

When I first went to Japan, everyone and their mama asked me if I had read *Memoirs of a Geisha*. I began to feel like the worst kind of ignoramus because I had not read Arthur Golden's best-selling book. But I was swamped with my work at *Newsweek* and my Japanese lessons took up all my free time. I packed *Memoirs of a Geisha* with me, and I read it in Kyoto, in a two-hundred-year-old inn near the geisha district. I walked the streets described in the novel by day. Then I stayed up for hours, traversing those same streets through the magic of Golden's prose at night. I am so grateful that I read *Memoirs of a Geisha* where I did and how I did.

We are constantly made to feel as if we were playing an infernal game of catch-up: what's hot at the box office, what's on the front page of the book review, where's the latest travel destination? Books will wait. Movies will wait. Languages will wait. And even countries will wait. Of course, there is a fine line between the joyful laziness of doing things in your own time and not doing anything at all. But I have always believed that if we stay alert to the possibilities, we will each be led to our own miracles, our own moments of grace.

When I first graduated from college, I read an article in a now-defunct magazine called *Mademoiselle* about women taking control of their finances. The article was by a writer named Lucy Schulte (now Lucy Danziger, the editor of *Self.*) At the time, I was making $18,000 a year and living in New York City, where rents and taxis and meals out were so expensive that I had no money to save or invest. But nonetheless I had been impressed with the quotes from a financial consultant named Linda Schoenthaler, and I carried that article around from purse to purse and from job to job. One day, I told myself, when I had money to save and invest, I was going to call her up.

Years went by, and the article began to fall apart. I made a photocopy and threw the original away. When that photocopy began to wither, I made three more. Placing one in a file and one in a purse and one in a desk drawer at the job I had at the time. Five years passed and finally, I was ready to make the move. Linda Schoenthaler no longer worked at the same firm. When I called, they told me she had opened her own firm on Madison Avenue. I called her new office and asked how much it was to see her. I later learned that she thought I was the dim-witted assistant of one of her competitors trying to inquire about her rates. She suggested I come in for an appointment if I was serious about hiring her. I went into her office that day with my mother, who happened to be visiting me from her home in Florida. The two of us were immediately impressed by the Madison Avenue digs. And this is what I remember more than anything, Linda's assistant offered us a cold drink, and two Coca-Colas quickly appeared on a silver tray, like something out of a movie. It was the first time that I'd ever experienced anything like that, and I was both excited and intimidated.

When I finally met Linda, she looked with disbelief at the five-year-old article I unfolded from my purse. And because I had been so determined to one day get my financial life on track, she offered to let me work with one of her junior associates at a rate that I could afford. I wish I could say this was how I built my fortune. Alas, I have no fortune. Not yet. But that day I took a powerful step from a life of credit card debt to a life of saving and investing. And I knew that step really began five years earlier, the day I ripped that article out of a magazine and refused to throw it away.

I know that a lot of people believe in visualization. But how does it work in real life? We visualize ourselves thin or rich or happy, but that doesn't necessarily make it so. When I was in my early twenties, I wandered—in a very haphazard way—onto a cliff, overlooking the Pacific

Ocean. Standing at the edge of this cliff and staring intently at the crashing waves was a legendary jazz musician that I had listened to my entire life. I introduced myself, and the jazz musician proceeded to tell me about a woman he had once dated, a famous actress, whom he seemed to still love even though it had been decades since the two had separated. "Beauty fades," the jazz musician said to me, "but substance doesn't. You think you are a grown woman, but you have hardly begun. Become a woman of substance." Then he gave me his phone number. I later found out that the woman he claimed to idolize he had also abused. But sometimes you have to know to take good advice from bad people, and his was still sound long after I misplaced his number.

The year I turned twenty-five turned out to be a miserable birthday for me. I broke up with my boyfriend and my best friend. My family life was in turmoil. My brother was in jail. My mother and I were at cross-purposes, stuck between our old roles and the kind of friendship of equals that we both wanted to have. I was lonely and tired, and I woke up each morning with the feeling that I'd spent the entire night being battered about beneath the sea. It was also the year of the O.J. Simpson trial, and the media think tank where I was a fellow kept asking me to go on television as a journalistic expert. I did not want to go on television and talk about O.J. Simpson, and the more I withdrew from the major news story of the year, the more I felt that I had failed in my work.

Earlier that year, I had been an editor at the *New York Times Magazine* and had bid, unsuccessfully, for the first serial rights to publish an excerpt from Frida Kahlo's illustrated journal. The drawings in that journal had stayed with me long after the auction to publish them had come and gone. I kept trying to figure out a way to use images in my own journal. Finally, shortly, after my twenty-fifth birthday, I decided to make a journal about the woman I wanted to be. I began to cut pictures out of magazines of women I admired. And what I realized was that the year I turned twenty-five, many of the women that I looked up to were actually turning thirty-seven. This must seem like a random discovery, but after a while, it began to gain credence. Emma Thompson was thirty-seven. And Angela Bassett was thirty-seven. And Kristin Scott Thomas was thirty-seven.

Ever since I was a teenager, I had dreamed of my twenty-fifth birthday. I had pictured myself a grown woman with my own apartment, having fabulous parties with my fabulous friends and a fabulous assortment of gentlemen callers. Truthfully? I stole this image straight from that swinging scene in *Breakfast at Tiffany's* where Holly Golightly crams a hundred guests into her bachelorette pad; at my party, too, somebody was going to wear a lampshade, and everyone would dance the samba until a tall model from Texas passed out facedown onto the floor. Since reality was quite the opposite, I picked the age of thirty-seven and began to make my first illustrated journal. I titled it "thirty-seven is the perfect age." I cut out pictures of women I admired with the soon-to-be-discarded rule that no one under thirty-seven could be in my "women of substance" journal. In this journal I wrote down why I admired these women and what steps I could take to get where they were at that age. Not only did I admire Emma Thompson for writing the screenplay for *Sense and Sensibility* but I admired Helen Mirren for being so comfortable in her own skin. I cut out pictures of Lena Horne, Charlotte Rampling, Oprah, and Joan Didion.

I once read that when you are having body-image problems you should go and visit the newborn ward at a hospital. Babies come in so many different sizes, so many different hair colors and eye colors and skin colors. And even the most odd-looking baby has the quality that the French called *jolie-laide*, so ugly that it is truly beautiful. As I made my illustrated journal of womanhood, I began to see that there are so many different ways to be what Maya Angelou calls a "phenomenal woman." I began to think about the kind of woman I wanted to be and I began to let go of the things that didn't matter. I didn't need to be drop-dead gorgeous, but admiring Angela Bassett clued

me into the fact that I wanted to be more than physically
fit. I wanted to be strong. I wanted to be multilingual like
Kristin Scott Thomas. I wanted to be well traveled like
Lauren Hutton. I began to "listen" to the women in my
journal, and the stories that they told me about my own
heart's desires began to astound me.

"Listen to your own heart," is the New Age mantra of
the day, but I have a heart that is very easily swayed. I
could have breakfast with a mentor, lunch with an old
friend, and dinner with a new paramour and be convinced
that each and every one of them had the perfect plan for
my life. Flipping through my "thirty-seven is the perfect
age" book has been a grounding tool because again and
again, I realized that things I want in my life never change:
wit and intelligence, a love of books, food, languages, and
travel. So when opportunities arose—a fellowship in
Japan, a writer's retreat in Maine—it was the journal that
I followed, not my own fickle head and heart.

My illustrated journal of womanhood has become a
gift not only to me but also to the women I know. When a
good friend of mine was on the eve of her thirty-seventh
birthday, she confessed to me that despite her enormous
professional success, she was frustrated. Her younger sister was happily married and my friend had no prospects
in sight. She wanted a family. I told her about my illustrated journal. "Thirty-seven is the perfect age," I told her.

She looked at me, soon to be married, and shook her head as if to say, "Nice try." I went to the old-fashioned copy shop in the town where I was living. I handed my journal to the older gentleman behind the counter. From the moment he opened his mouth, he was crotchety. Did I know how expensive color copies were? Did I know that you can't do two-sided copies in color? Did I know that he was not responsible if the pages of my journal were damaged? I told him that I did. He grumbled and shuffled toward the back, dismissing me with a wave and a guttural equivalent of "Bah, humbug."

When I returned, the man I met was a changed individual. He wanted me to know that he didn't mean to be all in my business, but that he thought the pages of my journal, decorated with pastels and crayons and colored pencils were "art." He looked at me, discerningly, "You're an artist." I thanked him, embarrassed and hopeful that my friend would feel the same way. I took the color pages from my journal and I pasted them carefully, into a blank leather-bound journal I had purchased for my friend's birthday. Then I sent them to her. The journal wasn't the charm I know, but I was happy to watch how, in that thirty-seventh year, her life came into bloom. She met and married the man of her dreams. Her tremendous professional success was topped by even greater success.

When we are children, we learn by repetition. We

copy everything down from the board and somewhere between the pencil in our hand and the gesture of writing, messages are sent to our brains, and those messages become knowledge. Similarly, as I cut out pictures for my illustrated journal, there is a line that is tethered between my fingertips and my heart. And it is on that line that I begin to transmit the knowledge that is etched in the faces of the women I admire. All along the way, I have been taping my own picture in the journal, mixed in with pictures of women whose substance I seek to emulate. I have lots of photo albums, but it's the pictures in my illustrated journal that move me the most. There are pictures of me that were taken for magazine articles and pictures of me that were taken by friends, when I wasn't looking. On my face I see the earnestness and wonder and hints of confidence that have been developing in my face for years. I place myself side by side, in my journal, with women like Jane Horrocks and Suzan Lori Parks and Sharon Olds, and I do not feel like I am less than they. Next to their pictures, I scribble their insights and my own opinions on work, marriage, motherhood, aging, friendship, failure, and success. When I flip through the book, what impresses me most is the array of wisdom gathered. I feel like I have taken the jazz musician's advice. I have become, in my heart, a woman of substance.

As I get older, I look forward to making more illustrated journals. Maybe the next one will be a "forty-four is
the perfect age" journal or a "fifty-two is the perfect age."
I am paying attention to the women who are older than I
am and waiting for inspiration to hit. Maybe my next
journal will begin with women in their sixties. As I write
this, Dame Judi Dench is about to turn sixty-nine. I love
Dame Dench. Watching back-to-back episodes of her old
BBC series *As Time Goes By* is my absolutely favorite way to
tuck myself into bed. It is the story of Jean, a widow who
falls back in love with a man she dated thirty-eight years
earlier. Geoffrey Palmer plays Lionel, her long-lost, now-
divorced love. For ten years, the show explored how Jean
and Lionel get reacquainted, forgive each other for past
transgressions, and decide to spend the rest of their lives
together. It is a grown-up fairy tale, and grown-up fairy
tales are my favorite, favorite thing. Perhaps I will one day
make an illustrated journal that begins with Judi Dench:
"sixty-nine is the perfect age." And I will sit at my table, as
I do now, with my crayons and colored pencils and
double-sided tape and stack of magazines, and I will imagine myself in that decade, drawing the best way I know
how, the sort of woman that I dream of becoming.

"I've never been interested in 'success,' which is so
ephemeral," Dench told an interviewer. "For me success

is having the respect and love of people who truly know you." But here's the gotcha: Who are the people who truly know you? Is it the family member who always sees you the way you were when you were a child? Talk to my cousin Guillermina, or my cousin Digna, or my beloved aunt Diana, and they will tell you that I am a barrel of nerves. For them, the quintessential Veronica story took place the day I was nine and I decided to pour myself a cup of tea. My hands quivering, I lost control of the teapot and proceeded to pour boiling water all over my lap. When my cousins or my aunt call me and I'm busy or when I am driving them around in my car—and even on the day that I got married—they do not see me as I am now. They see me as I was then. To them, I am always just about to pour boiling water on my own lap.

Who are the people who truly know you? Is it the boss who passes you over for a promotion, who notices every detail that you miss—does he or she see inside you and glimpse the limitations that your loved ones are too blind to catch? Does your spouse know you? Your children? Your nearest and dearest friends? They say if you were to send twelve photographers into a perfectly empty white room, they would emerge with twelve different photographs. I know if I were to ask twelve people who know me to tell me what they see, not only would they tell me twelve different things, they would tell me a few things I really don't want to know.

Flatter me. Tell me gentle and bold-faced lies. As I get older, I am becoming fonder of tenderness. This wasn't always the case. I remember as a college freshman that I wanted only the hardest teachers I could find. I figured that if I started out with the most exacting, my work would reach a level that would carry me through all four years. As it was, this worked out well for me. I graduated summa cum laude, in large part, because of the way my freshman year professors kicked my butt. I developed discipline and good study habits, and my internal bar was set very high. After college, I took on tough assignments at work and played the martyr with friends who constantly needed saving and sought out the most impossible men to love. There is an expression in Spanish that I have often heard other Latinas use: "*La vida es duro, pero yo soy más duro.*" Translated, it means, "Life is tough, but I am tougher." It used to be my mantra, it's not anymore.

These days, I have no interest in proving how tough I am and in as much as I get to choose how I view life, give me *la vie en rose*, life seen through rose-tinted glasses. With my friends and family, I increasingly seek the love and respect of people who make me feel good. Sometimes I fear that this veers dangerously close into the territory of wanting to be around only people who tell me what I want to hear. This may be the case, but does it matter? I want friends who laugh at my jokes and who think I'm fashionable and smart and fabulous. My husband is constantly telling me how sexy and beautiful he thinks I am. I used to dismiss these compliments out of hand, literally brushing them away with my hands. Recently, I have begun the long, slow road of trying to lose the twenty pounds I have gained in the last year and a half. I've been working out with a running coach, training for a half marathon, and going to the gym four to six days a week. After two months of studiously avoiding the scale— "muscle weighs more than fat!" my trainer kept telling me—I hopped on the terror machine/scale at my gym. And I discovered that I hadn't lost a single pound. I wanted to fall down crying; and, of course, it seemed that every other woman in the locker room was svelte, model thin. But then I remembered how my husband's eyes light up each and every time I walk into the room—I took a shower and let him take me out on the town, and I did not mention my weight, even once. I know that I am successful in my marriage, not because I have a crystal ball and believe it will last forever, but because I am married to a man who is so committed to building me up. Perhaps this is what Dame Judi Dench means when she says that success is having the love and respect of people who truly know you. Maybe by people who truly know you, she means people who are invested in building you up instead of cutting you down.

~

It's no secret that I cannot sing. I have a voice that could peel paint off the walls. For a long time, I hid this flaw, embarrassed. I willed myself to silence when a favorite song came on the radio, lip-synched "Happy Birthday" whenever somebody brought out a cake. In church, where voices were ablaze with praise songs that I loved, I imagined that some other woman's sweet soprano was coming out of my mouth. "Getting happy off of someone else's sound" was what I called it.

One Sunday morning I was pressing my lips shut and clapping my hands when the minister sidled up next to me. "Why aren't you singing?" he asked. "I can't sing," I whispered to him, afraid of attracting too much attention. "I have an awful voice." Then the minister looked at me and said five of the most beautiful words I have ever heard. He said, "Do you think God cares?"

Ever since that glorious day, my love for singing has grown exponentially. I sing in the shower and around the house. I sing in the car, at church, and on the dance floor. The DJ who plays Gloria Gaynor is just asking for me to

put a hurting on "I Will Survive." We are told that practice makes perfect, but the truth is no amount of practice
will improve my singing. But my singing, wretched as it
may be, has vastly improved my living. "I want to tell you
something but I don't want you to be offended," Jason, my
then fiancé, told me as we washed the dinner dishes and I
crooned along to Ella Fitzgerald. "The thing I love about
you is that your singing is so wretched but you do it anyway." His backhanded compliment confirmed not only
why I married him but a truth I had long suspected. The
things we do badly set us apart; what we consider our failures have a surprising ability to charm. We think we have
to be perfect for other people to love us, when in fact the
opposite is true. We are loved for our imperfections—for
our funny faces and walks and dances and songs.

PART I

Gut Instincts

1

What I've Learned from Julia Child

ON THE SATURDAY FOLLOWING JULIA CHILD'S DEATH, I was in the bathroom of a restaurant and I overheard the following conversation. The woman in the first stall said, "I'm so stupid. I tried to make myself a piece of salmon for dinner and I had no idea what to do. So I put it in the pan to sauté it, but I hadn't put any oil in so it all stuck to the pan. I didn't know how long to cook it, so I let it cook until it was practically burned!" The woman in the second stall said, "No big deal! Did you know that Julia Child didn't learn how to cook until she was thirty-six years old?" The first woman, the salmon torcher, emerged from the stall with a huge smile on her face. "I'll be thirty-five on my next birthday," she said. Her friend emerged from the stall next to her and said, "See, you could be the next Julia Child. You could change the face of cooking."

The whole conversation made me smile because it was indicative of so many things that I've been thinking about: How we beat ourselves up over the tiniest things, about the primal role food plays in our lives, and how much Julia Child has taught us not only about food but also about life. It seems like the older we get, the higher the bar is raised. I remember, as a child, being so impressed by all the whiz kids that I'd read about in the news: gymnasts and ballet dancers, chess players and piano prodigies. I honestly remember thinking, at the age of eleven, that if only I applied myself then maybe I could do something with my life! Even when I ended up going to college at the age of sixteen, I still felt only average. At the early college I attended, half of the college freshmen were fifteen. The year I started college, there were two fourteen-year-old freshmen and one who was just thirteen. At sixteen, I was practically a remedial first-year college student!

Julia Child's *The Way to Cook* has been a staple of my adult life. I turn to it the way I imagine that a 1950s housewife would ring up her mother. How do you steam an artichoke? How long do you boil an ear of corn? What exactly does it mean to poach a piece of fish? Whenever a direction in a recipe was puzzling, I opened *The Way to Cook* and "asked" Julia. In the months since Julia Child passed away, I've been digging into her life and learning about more than cooking. "When the student is ready, the teacher will appear" is an old Zen saying. And as I get into the thick of my thirties—the years when Julia Child got married, learned how to cook, found her true calling—I'm assured that the wisdom of the Zen saying is true. Piano prodigies and Russian gymnasts be damned, I love the idea that for both myself and the girl I overheard in the bathroom, the ride, the real roller coaster ride of life, is just about to begin. So in the unscientific and unflinchingly honest way that she heralded, here are just a few of the things that I have learned from Julia Child.

Lesson 1: Hang on to your friends.

Long before she taught the world how to cook and became in the manner of all great personalities, the kind of figure that a million strangers thought of as a friend, Julia Child was the center of a vibrant social circle. Rosemary Mannell, who served as a kind of sous chef on Julia's first public television show, *The French Chef,* had known Julia and her husband since 1949 when they all lived in France. Paul Child and Rosemary's husband, Abram, were in the Foreign Service together. The two couples became a sort of gourmet club, getting together for frequent dinners at the Childs' apartment on the Rue de l'Université or at the Mannells' on the Ile St-Louis. Elizabeth Bishop, another one of the sous chefs on Julia's show, once told a friend, "Cooking is the least of it. You know, in a funny way, I feel closer to Julia than I do to anyone. Of course, I'm *closer* to Jack [Bishop] and the children, but there are things I could say to her that I couldn't say to anyone else."

There were other friends. Simca Beck and Louisette Bertholle, with whom Julia started Les Ecole de Trois Gourmands, the small, private cooking school that they ran out of the Childs' Paris apartment. There was Avis De-Voto, who served as an informal editor for Julia's first, groundbreaking book. "We both liked to write letters," DeVoto told an interviewer. "There was a lot to write about. The McCarthy thing was heating up in Washington. Julia and Paul were both rather frightened by it. Sometimes we'd write each other three or four times a week."

I love this, because I am so over e-mail. At any given time, I find myself fifty to a hundred messages behind. If

I am especially busy, my in-box swells to five hundred, and it becomes impossible for me to pick out the wheat—a missive from a beloved friend, news of a baby born or a new job, or a fond "remember when"—from all the chaff, the department store sale updates, the sure-fire investment advice, and offers for Internet porn. I try to write letters because I like getting something in the mail besides bills and junk, and I imagine that my friends feel the same. I try to send paper birthday cards for the same reason. I water the gardens of my relationships the best way I know how because, like Julia, I want to have fifty-year-old friendships one day.

What to do, though, about the weeding of such gardens? I cannot let a friendship go. Do not ask me to do it. Sometimes, when I get to the point where I know a friendship must end but I am too jelly-bellied to do it, the universe performs the amputation for me. I move or my friend moves, and there are no hard feelings. But sometimes, a friendship lingers on and on and then what to do?

There is no manual for breaking up with a friend. Therapists, religious leaders, wise women, and elders guide us through the dissolution of romantic relationships and marriage, but there is no high court of friendship to legally and permanently break its bonds. Without this guidance, the ailing friendships in my life break up in fits of pent-up fury and frustration. In the last ten years, I have broken up with—or been dumped by—three dear friends. Every case involved tears; hundreds of dollars' worth of therapy; a film festival of sappy chick flicks; and an elementary school girl's conviction that if I were prettier, more popular, and less of a "super freak," the friendship would still be intact. This tremendously mature life view has been highlighted only by the fact that I am highly resistant to change. At every social gathering, my internal MP3 player blasts the same track over and over again: "No new friends. No new friends." Honestly, I never got the whole "Make new friends, but keep the old. One is silver, and the other's gold" business. Who wants silver when you've got gold?

Lately though, I have been wondering whether this passion I have for my old friends, as flawed as each one of us may be, could be chalked up to something more than my being bullheaded and stubborn. The older I get, the more I value my friends as witnesses to the girl I once was and the young woman I'll never be again. As my life becomes more settled, I want to look into a friend's eyes and see the me that danced on top of bars, drove a convertible through the desert in Mexico, and unabashedly wore blue eye shadow on my chocolate brown skin. As I become increasingly comfortable with a certain level of success, I want to hold on to the friends who know how hard I worked to get here, the ones who stop me mid-sentence when my humility veers into a kind of disingenuous, self-flagellating deprecation.

I look around my apartment at the gifts my friends have given me. Treasured books that represent shared passions like Laurie King's *The Beekeeper's Apprentice,* recipes scrawled in familiar handwriting, Depression-era glass found by a friend who has an eye for such things—and I do not want the objects I own to outlast the friendships they sprung from. Which is why during a recent break-up with a friend, I decided no, I could not, did not, want to lose this friend. Maybe we won't pal around every weekend, maybe we shouldn't send e-mail every day. But I don't want to drive the long way around her house. I don't want to clench my teeth when mutual acquaintances mention her name. She is one of the funniest, smartest, most engaging people I know. And more. To quote Alice Munro, she is a friend of my youth. I want to know her. I want to keep getting to know her, even if it's from the polite distance of a semiannual cup of tea. I want to be in my nineties, like Julia Child, and be able to reminisce with this woman about the lives that we lived. We may not always get along in the present, but I have never not been fascinated by her stories, her jokes, the way she views the world. So I called her, and I begged her. We are two yolks poured into a bowl, I said. Please. Don't ask me to unbeat this egg.

Lesson 2: Laughter makes a woman beautiful.

Julia Child was born Julia McWilliams, in Pasadena, in 1912, to a family of California landowners. Like so many well-heeled girls of her age, she attended Smith College, the women's college. Her mother had been in Smith's class of 1900. Julia entered in 1934, with the vague aspiration of becoming a novelist and a perhaps unstated understanding that her ultimate degree would be an "Mrs." She wrote for the college newspaper, then moved to New York, where she took a job at an advertising firm. "I had a very good time doing virtually nothing," she has said of this time. "There was always lots of fun and laughter." I can imagine Julia carousing around New York in the 1930s to a soundtrack from a Cole Porter musical. Fun and laughter; it's free, it's magical, but it requires effort.

I've known so many miserable people. I have one friend who, whenever I call her, sounds like the somber receptionist at a very busy funeral home. "Hi, how are you?" I say. "Oh, I'm working," she says, in a voice that seems to imply that her work involves the unearthing of small bones in a mass grave in a war-torn land. This particular friend, in fact, has quite a nice job that I happen to know she loves, at an entertainment law firm. Call her at home, and the tone is no different. "Hi, what are you up to this weekend?" I might ask her. "Oh, I'm going to a party," she says. And the tone in her voice implies that she is a soothsayer being lured onto the *Titanic*.

Full disclosure. I am not a big fan of the phone. Call me at any given time, and I'm liable to answer the phone sounding like the Madwoman of Chaillot: hurried or morose but every once in a while, giggly. (I have a joke with an old friend: When we know it is the other person calling, we answer, "House of Beauty. This is Cutie.") At the same time, I've learned that joy is in the small things: how I answer the phone, how I greet the security guard at my office, how I ride up and down the elevator in my building. In every single moment, every single hour, every single day, I can make the decision to be happy or not. So if I'm having a crap day at work, I can choose to be miserable on the phone or I can be happy that I am on the phone with someone I like—as opposed to in an infernally long meeting with the weasel in accounting—and I can settle into the call and enjoy myself. "Happiness is equilibrium," Tom Stoppard wrote. "Shift your weight."

Scientists say that a smile, even forced or fake, sends a certain happy message to the brain. Sometimes when I am fighting the mean reds, I sit in my office or my kitchen or my bedroom and I smile. If a smile is the happiness equivalent of a cup of coffee, then laughter is a double-shot of espresso. I love it when a friend calls or my husband sends me an e-mail with a funny article and I laugh out loud. "Thank you," I call and tell them. "That was my first laugh of the day." That kind of belly laugh makes me feel lucky, like a gambler whose horse has come out on top at the races. Laughter is the best face lift, says the French writer Veronique Vienne, and when we watched Julia Child (or her British heir-apparent, Nigella Lawson) we're reminded: Laughter makes a woman beautiful.

When I was single and shy, I discovered that I laughed only around my friends. I was working in New York as a journalist and was often invited to swank parties, movie screenings and book launches, and parties at such legendary places as the U.N. and the Rainbow Room. I often met interesting, fascinating men but seemed unable to get them to ask me out. Of course, I thought that this was because I was not pretty, interesting, or fascinating enough. One day, my friend Cassandra, who is a guru of charm and fashion, looked me up and down with a very critical eye. "Have you ever noticed that when you meet a man you like, you scowl?" I was sure she was kidding. "Yes, you scowl. It's as if you were studying for a test." That night, I went home and looked in the bathroom mirror, imagining that I was engrossed in a deep conversation with, say, Kofi Annan. The expression on my face, which I had always imagined to be soft and slightly thoughtful, was actually pained and slightly worried. Some women brood beautifully—Nicole Kidman, Dorothy Dandridge, Ingrid Bergman. I am not, as it turns out, one of those women.

I went back to Cassandra. "You are so right," I told her. "What do I do?" She told me that when I meet a man I like, I should smile. "If he's across the room, then wink," she advised. This filled me with a kind of abject fear. Winking has never been my strong suit. I can only wink with one eye and it is not a sultry, effortless wink. It is the full-faced wink of a Little Rascal sending a message of mischief to one of his Little Rascal friends. Cassandra said that all I needed to do was practice.

It was during this same conversation, getting ready to go out to dinner one night, that Cassandra noticed how haphazardly I was putting on my makeup. "Your face is a canvas," she said. "You have to treat it like a painting." I explained that I never wore much makeup: a little eyeshadow, mascara, some face powder, lipstick and I am done. "Yes," she said. "But doing those four things should take you more than two minutes." She was right. I barreled through the whole routine. Cassandra suggested I put on some music, take my time, pour myself a glass of wine, and enjoy the process. "Practice doing your makeup when you're not going out, take your time," she advised. This is how, one Sunday evening, my friend Michael came over to find me in sweats and full makeup. "Are you going out?" he wondered. No, I told him, I was practicing my makeup.

Practicing my winking turned out to be a much harder thing to do. Mostly because winking makes me feel stupid. Then, one day, I was having breakfast at a hotel in South Africa. I had noticed this man from the moment I entered the hotel restaurant. He had a friendly, familiar face that immediately put me at ease. I went ahead and had breakfast, then as I was leaving, I decided, what the hell? I was a gazillion miles away from home. I did not know a soul in this country. I was going to wink at him. Nine in the morning is a little early to be playing the coquette, but I decided to test my courage. I caught his eye, and he smiled back. I took a deep breath, winked, and proceeded to fall down the stairs. There were only four steps, but I hadn't seen them coming and now, post wink, I was lying in a pile of embarrassment at the bottom of the stairs. Mortified. I wanted to get up, but I was surrounded by hotel staff, ordering me not to move. The hotel manager appeared, asking me to sign a release saying that the fall had been entirely my fault. I was dizzy with embarrassment and the confusion of the surrounding lawsuit-wary staff. Then suddenly the man appeared. "Somebody should call a doctor," one of the staff members finally said. The cause of my affliction then said the most movielike thing I'd ever heard off screen: "I am a doctor." He was not feeding me a line. He was an M.D. That night, and every night afterward for the remainder of my trip, the good doctor took me out to dinner. And each night, we laughed about the wink that landed me on my butt and in the seat next to him at the dinner table. On the airplane ride home, I knew that while I had not met the love of my life, something deep in my life had shifted. I had made an utter fool of myself and in the process, I had met a gorgeous and funny man.

I do not know if it was Julia Child's robust laugh that attracted her husband, Paul. I do know that after her advertising stint in New York, Julia volunteered for overseas duty with the Office of Strategic Services. It was the middle of World War II and an adventurous Julia McWilliams signed up for a tour of duty in Asia. She took a train across the United States, a boat to Australia and another boat to Bombay, before landing in Ceylon where she met Paul. This leads me to the next thing that I have learned from Julia Child.

Lesson 3: Travel—it's always worth it.
Waiting for love—also worth it.

In Ceylon, Paul Child was in charge of visual presentation: maps, charts, troop concentrations, and all the paraphernalia of military planning. Julia worked in the registry, sending messages to and from O.S.S. field agents. Paul was ten years older than Julia and had already seen a lot of the world. In New Delhi, he'd set up the war room for Lord Louis Mountbatten. He'd been an artist in Paris, hanging out with Gertrude Stein and Ernest Hemingway. He'd been a lumberman in Maine and a waiter in Hollywood. He was also becoming a bachelor of legendary note. But Julia McWilliams caught his attention. "She seemed like a pretty, great woman to me," he has said. "She was completely competent, unflappable and running a very complicated operation with great skill." When both Paul Child and Julia McWilliams were later deployed to Kunming, China, a romance blossomed. They were married in 1946. Julia was thirty-four, a veritable old maid by the standards of that era.

I was thirty-one the year that I got married. Although it seemed to me that I had been perpetually and was perhaps, terminally, unlucky in love, thirty-one is not so far above the national standard when it comes to getting married. In New York, where I was living at the time, my age was actually below the standard. As *Sex and the City*'s Carrie Bradshaw so memorably showed us, who needs to get married when you are surrounded by great friends and hopelessly in love with a city like New York? Still, when I was single and lonely, the time between boyfriends seemed interminable. What I learned from Julia Child and all the women adventurers that I have admired—Margaret Bourke-White, Georgia O'Keeffe, Amelia Earhart—is that you have to have your own life. For me, like Julia Child, that has always involved travel.

When I graduated from college, I was offered a job for the princely sum of $21,000. This offer was made to me by human resources. When the woman I would actually be working for heard of the sum, she threw a fit. When she had graduated from college, a few years before, she had made only $15,000 a year. Human resources came back to me with an offer I so badly wanted to refuse: the same job, at $18,000 a year. That year, the country was experiencing a terrible recession. So many people I knew were being laid off, and many of my friends were applying to graduate school with the hopes of deferring both their student loans and what seemed like imminent unemployment. It rained a lot that spring, and I remember going from job interview to job interview in my one nice dress, arriving at each location soaked to the gills. It was a cold and rainy day when human resources called and told me that they

were knocking $3,000 off of my starting salary. "No prob-
lem," I chirped happily into the phone. "I'll take it."

That year, I decided that every year I would take one
domestic trip and one international trip. If you are in possession of even the most basic math skills, you can understand how on a salary of $18,000 and paying rent in New
York City, that there really was no money for me to travel
anywhere. Still, armed with credit cards and convinced
that money spent traveling was "good debt," I kept my
promise to myself and I traveled. Over the next few years
I went to California and to London. I went on a photography trip to Morocco and a weekend biking trip to Block
Island, Rhode Island. I went to South Africa, and when
three months later a good friend moved to China, I said
"what the hell" and joined her in Shanghai. It took me
more than five years of hard work and moonlighting to
wipe out all that "good debt" but I do not regret it.

The first date I had with my husband, I pretended to
be something that I am not. He ordered a martini. And in
a ridiculous effort to seem like Kate Spade (house in the
Hamptons, alligator handbag, and stiletto-heel cute), I ordered a martini too. I am not a good liar, and the look on
my face made it clear that not only did I hate the taste of a
vodka martini but I'd never had one before in my life. I
looked at my future husband and confessed, "I drink only

sweet drinks," and then I turned to the bartender and asked for the girliest drink he could concoct.

As the evening wore on and I happily sipped a pomegranate margarita, the one thing that I did not have to fake was my love of travel. On that first date, Jason and I talked about books and movies and music. But what was electric between us was our love of travel. We talked about the cities we loved in common: Paris, of course, London, too. Then we talked about the cities that were not mutual friends. Jason told me about his time in St. Petersburg and Budapest and Plovdiv. I talked about Shanghai and Capetown and Tokyo. "Marry a man who wants the same kind of life you do," my friend Jenny Bevill once told me. And although I did not know that night that Jason and I would get married, certainly I knew that I'd met a fellow gypsy. We talked and talked that night from cocktails at one place to dinner and dessert at another. And when the bill came, I did not want to stop talking. So Jason walked me home, from Tribeca across the Brooklyn Bridge to my front stoop on State Street in Brooklyn Heights. Sometimes I feel that our entire relationship has been one long extended conversation that began that night, and has so far carried us in our travels from Brooklyn to Princeton to Philadelphia to Maine to the Bahamas to London to Paris to Lake Como to Tokyo to Barcelona and Madrid and

Granada to Tokyo and Sapporo and Toronto and Montreal
to Los Angeles, where I'm writing from now.

In the course of their courtship and subsequent marriage,
Paul and Julia Child lived in Ceylon, Kunming, Washington, Paris, Marseilles, Oslo, Bonn, and Boston. They eventually settled in Cambridge, with a second home in the
south of France. It is not the model for every marriage, although it is one that Jason and I would love to emulate.
What is the model, I believe, are the details of Julia's womanhood. Julia having a life of her own as a single girl in
New York. Julia taking a chance and moving to India, in
the middle of a world war. Julia not settling, not worry-
ing about when she would get married and doing it, as she
did almost everything, in her own sweet time—with glorious gusto and a great dose of joy. Nobody can tell you
how to be a woman with a rich and wonderful life. I, for
one, find the whole business of "you'll have to figure it out
on your own" really frustrating. I want womanhood to be
like second grade. I want stations for coloring and finger
painting and reading. I want brightly colored boxes and a
teacher and bells that ring throughout the day. And more
than anything else, I want my name on a bulletin board at

the back of the room. My name, trailed by a long line of gold stars for penmanship and sportsmanship, reading and mathematics. I know there's no report card, no list of school supplies to check off for this enterprise of a life well lived. But I look at the life of Julia Child, and I see the outlines of a list. Laughter—check. Independence—check. Courage—check. Passport—check. Love—check, check, check, gold star.

∞

VERONICA'S QUICKIE COQ AU VIN HOMAGE TO JULIA CHILD

I love everything about Julia Child. But I am lazy in my admiration. Her coq au vin recipe requires more than twenty ingredients. Mine requires six (not including spices). Hers takes ninety minutes, conservatively. Mine takes half an hour. If you're a novice cook or short on time, I suggest you try mine. As long as you serve it on a pretty plate with a nice glass of wine, I'm sure that Julia wouldn't mind.

4 SERVINGS

2 chicken breast halves (I like boneless)

4 ounces shiitake mushrooms

2 tablespoons olive oil

1 packet garlic and herb salad dressing mix
   (such as Good Seasons)

1 cup frozen small onions, thawed

2 cups red wine

Preheat the oven to 375°F. Marinate the chicken breasts in one cup red wine and whatever spices you have on hand that taste good (I like sea salt, pepper, garlic, thyme, dried shallots—but just salt and pepper is fine). Heat olive oil in a large, oven-proof casserole, and sear the chicken, skin-side down, for two minutes. Place dish in the oven, cook chicken for five minutes, turn, then cook for five more minutes. Remove chicken from casserole dish. Back on the stovetop, add the mushrooms (you may need a little more oil) over medium high heat. Add, stirring in, in order: onions, salad dressing mix, wine, and chicken broth. Add the chicken, cover, and simmer over low heat for fifteen minutes. (Turn chicken halfway through.) Remove chicken, mushrooms, and onions. Increase the heat until the sauce is boiling (maybe add a little more wine), reduce until the sauce has thickened, and pour it over the chicken and vegetables.

Everyday Picnic

N ONE OF MY FAVORITE BOOKS, *Everyday Sacred*, author
Sue Bender uses bowls as a metaphor for gratitude. She
tells, for example, the story of a monk and his begging
bowl. The monk goes out with his bowl, and whatever is
placed in the bowl is his nourishment for his day. Sue Bender urges us to think of our day like the monk's bowl:
Whatever happens in our day, whatever is placed in our
"bowl"—good or bad—is our nourishment for the day.

For me, picnic baskets have a similar sort of magic as

Sue Bender's bowls; they have the power to transform the ordinary into the extraordinary. A tuna fish sandwich is just a tuna fish sandwich, but stick it in a picnic basket with a soft drink and some checkered paper napkins and all of a sudden, the meal is elevated. "Use the good sheets," my friend Diana used to say as a way of reminding me to live each day to its fullest, to stop hoarding the good stuff for occasions so special they never actually come. Picnic baskets are my way of reminding myself that every day is an occasion worthy of celebrating—and that if I can't find a reason to celebrate, then I need to stop, breathe, and take a minute to be grateful.

Now that I live in California, I picnic more than I ever have before. My husband hates my picnic basket, it's wooden and vintage (in other words, it's bulky). Sometimes, he doesn't understand why we can't just carry our sandwiches in a nice, disposable plastic bag. For him, a picnic basket is much ado about nothing. But I spend most of my days and many of my nights hustling and bustling. Packing a picnic basket is my way—one of the few ways I know—of hitting the pause button.

My favorite picnic memory is not actually my own. In my mind, the perfect picnic would be à la Audrey Hepburn and Albert Finney, motoring through the French countryside in a scene out of the movie *Two for the Road*. In real life, the very notion of organizing a picnic seems to throw my friends into a panic. Who has the time (or ability) to fry chicken so delicious it tastes good cold? Who wants to get stuck eating soggy sandwiches? How do you fend off ants and avoid such mood-killers as too-warm wine and the inevitable grass stain on your new white jeans?

It has been five centuries since the French introduced the world to the idea of the *pique-nique*. And like so many things that the French pioneered, a *pique-nique* is not as effortless as it seems. The British shunned the idea of carrying a basket of food into the woods or onto the field until 1800. And even then, the bar was set high. In the nineteenth-century tome *Book of Household Management*, one Mrs. Beeton let it be known that to pull off a true picnic, the host must serve no fewer than thirty different dishes. In America, where we know how to relax the rules, picnics have disintegrated into a hodgepodge of lukewarm food that should have been served hot and hot foods that were meant to be served cold. Long drives in the car and an old-fashioned picnic basket with no insulation led to countless cases of mild food poisoning. Almost everyone I know remembers a picnic with mediocre food and the mysterious stomach ailments that followed.

But still we persist in our pursuit of the *pique-nique*. If we are to embrace the joy of doing things badly, then *c'est necessaire*. I am interested in picnics because they are an emblem of optimism. When life's a picnic, then things are good.

It is probably no accident that my dining room table is actually a picnic table—a long, wooden plank recovered (or so I was told) from a European farmhouse. There are no chairs, just wooden benches, polished dark brown with beeswax. Jason and I bought the table after much Sturm und Drang, e-mails back and forth to the antiques shop in California, long and slightly heated discussions about whether the cost of the table had been inflated in proportion to its supposed European origins. In the end, we had to have it. A picnic table in our dining room, we reasoned, would make it feel like summer all year long. So we paid for the European farmhouse lore and we paid to have the table shipped from Los Angeles to Philadelphia. Then, quite unexpectedly, three months later, my husband was transferred to his Los Angeles office. So we paid to have the table shipped back.

Our first home in Los Angeles was in Venice, near the beach. Our dining area opened through a pair of French doors onto a patio. We had no money, and I hated the idea of going into hock for patio furniture when chances were good, excellent even, that we would be moving again. So when the weather was nice, we moved our picnic table outdoors and ate out there. Seeing the table outside, under a canopy of trees, I could not help but think that moving it outside was the furniture equivalent of *Born Free*. Alas, there is the business of its European pedigree, and the mahogany stain. So while we moved the picnic table outside on occasion, we always dragged it back into captivity at the end of the evening.

Our hunch that another move was in the works proved to be correct. We are now in a condo building on the other side of town. As ours is the sixth floor unit, the picnic table is firmly ensconced in our dining room. Since we've moved into our new digs, I've had many the persnickety guest comment on our informal dining table. Said guest usually says, "I like your table, it has a certain rustic charm. But I do not like the benches. You should really get some chairs." But Jason and I love the intimacy of sitting on a bench while we eat. Benches are relaxed. And when we have dinner parties, we find that the ice breaks faster when the guests are sitting cheek to cheek. A chef once told me that every great dinner begins with something you can eat with your hands: shrimp cocktail, popcorn shrimp, pigs in the blanket. "When you eat with your hands, you feel like a child, which subconsciously makes you happier," he said. Even after hours of sitting at the table, our guests never want to move into our living room. I think they like our picnic table and the benches because it makes them feel like children, full and tired, splayed out in the playground.

Picnics are a ritual of summer. It has been ten plus years since I was last a student, but I still cling to the school year calendar. For me, fall feels like the beginning of the year. Ideally, I would like to take the time, every September, to buy myself some back-to-school clothes and make a run to Staples for an organizer, a box of my favorite pens, and maybe a new journal. People always ask me if I write in a journal every day. They imagine that because I'm a writer, writing in a journal must be like a pianist practicing. My lofty answer is that writing is only a small part of my job, the bigger part of my job is actually reading, observing, and researching. My not so lofty answer is that like everybody else, I am often too busy to write in my journal. I am happy, thrilled really, when I can write my thoughts down once a week. But sometimes months go by without my scribbling an intimate, personal word. When I was first starting to jog, I asked a woman I knew if she ran every day. She said, "I don't. But it's always a better day when I do." I feel the same way about journal writing. I'm clearer, less desperate for turbo sessions of therapy and the subliminal "reward" of cupcakes when I take the time to sit and write and pay attention to my thoughts.

Journals and new clothes are back to school. What about the rituals of winter? For a very long time, I practically hibernated during the winter, rushing to work, then rushing home to get out of the cold. Then I read an article about light therapy that stressed the importance of spending time outside in the colder months. The article also had what struck me as a very novel suggestion: Bundle up and go for a walk. At the time, I did not own a pair of long johns. So I bought some. I put on a pair of tights and an undershirt, then my long johns and a pair of jeans, two pairs of socks, a heavy sweater, and my winter coat. I wore a hat even though, in my vanity, I avoided winter hats at all costs, put on a pair of gloves, and went out for a walk. I had not been so well dressed for the cold weather since I was a kid and my mother dressed me to go out and play. The walk was wonderful, and I've yet to think of winter in a depressed way again. If I hadn't learned the importance of winter sunlight, I would have never found myself one Christmas morning in Paris, lacing up my sneakers for a run to the Luxembourg Gardens. It is one of my favorite holiday memories, the sun shining bright, the *thump, thump, thump* of my feet dashing past the regal apartment buildings and charming shops of the sixth arrondissement.

I am a flower fanatic, so every spring feels like God keeping a promise He has been making with me all winter long. In Brooklyn, where I was born and lived most of my adult life, my favorite florist is Seaport Florists in Brooklyn Heights. The girls at that shop, especially Jane, the owner, and Felicia, a pal, have known me for more than ten years. When there was a choice between a cart full of groceries or my weekly visit to Seaport, I always chose the flowers. In New York, you can always eat cheaply: ramen noodles and falafel or, for three dollars, a slice of pizza and a soda at an old-fashioned pizzeria. The more money I had, the more flowers I bought. I loved Seaport because I could always trust that the flowers there, while not cheap, would last and fill my apartment with the fragrances of a Parisian market. In turn, the owners kept an eye on me. Once, when I returned early from a business trip, they glanced up at the calendar and said, "You're not supposed to be back for three days." In the years when I was the last member of my immediate family to live in Brooklyn, and many of my friends lived across the river in Manhattan, Seaport Florists was an extension of my home.

When my husband and I first met, he decided to send me flowers before our third date. At the time, he lived in Philadelphia. He received a recommendation from a co-worker for three florists in New York. On a whim, he called the girls at Seaport, unaware that it was my favorite florist. When he gave them my name, they asked him in a business-like fashion whether these should be sent to my work or home. Flustered, he asked how many men were in the habit of sending me flowers. He ordered the flowers anyway, and the girls took special care to give me exactly what they knew I'd want. I could not have chosen a better bouquet myself, and it was with my nose pressed into those fragrant petals that I began to fall for my husband in a way that I took great pains to hide. Throughout our courtship—for my birthday, for dinner parties, and holidays—Jason would surprise me with a bouquet, each more exquisite than the last.

For years, I had felt a certain sort of loneliness going to Seaport. I was happy to buy myself flowers, happy that I had the confidence to treat myself well, happy that I had the means. But some of the arrangements that I bought there were salves, metaphorically pressed against the places where my heart ached. I never imagined that a man would fall in love with me and use flowers to woo me. I am not a gardener, but I guess this is the nature of spring. I had planted the seeds, all those years of buying flowers for myself. It only made sense that one day, when the winter ended, spring and love would bloom for me within Seaport's four walls.

Which brings me back to summer; I have not had a summer off since I was in school. A week of vacation here and there hardly does it. In some of the jobs I have held, including the one I currently hold, summer vacations are not allowed at all. This year, I took a vacation in April and May. These were wonderful vacations: a week in Tokyo with my husband, a week at a spa with a girlfriend. But still come July, I find myself in an office with a window that doesn't open, and I'm all of a sudden in the summer-school detention room I'd avoided throughout my childhood. It is summer school with a paycheck, but it feels like summer school all the same. Over the past ten years, there have been whole summers when I did not go to the beach or eat a hot dog at a backyard barbecue or even paint my toes some fabulous sandal-worthy color. I don't want to live like that anymore. So I have been making a concentrated effort to use my free time to connect with the rituals of the season.

One of the happiest days of my life involved a picnic of sorts. Jason and I were still living in Venice, California. We got up early on a Sunday morning and drove to Runyon Canyon where we went on an hour-long hike. Then we came home, showered, and changed into our swimsuits. We took the newspaper and a blanket and walked down to the beach. We weren't wearing watches, but after a few hours, we decided it must be dinner time. We stopped at our favorite cheese shop, Stroh's on Abbot Kinney. We bought a baguette, some blue cheese, dried sausage, and some fruit. We brought it all home and were shocked when we got there to find out that we'd been to the mountains and we'd been to the beach and it was only four o'clock in the afternoon. It seemed like we must have fallen down Alice's rabbit hole. All week long, it seems like there is never enough time, that there are too few hours in the day. But on this Sunday, time seemed to expand. We were lottery winners, swimming in a pool of free time. So we sat on our deck, opened a bottle of wine and ate our picnic supper, talking and talking until the sun finally set.

The last time my friends and I had a picnic, it rained (of course) and we stood under an awning with our bags of gourmet sandwiches and our bottle of wine waiting for the weather to clear. When, finally, the rain let up, the grass was wet and the person who brought the blanket had brought one that was too nice to get soggy. So we laid out our feast on a park bench, and we stood around, juggling plates and chatting like we were at a cocktail party. In memory, picnics are perfect. In real life, a nice café with an outdoor patio seems like the more civilized option.

All summer long, Jason and I have been "picnicking" in the garden of our apartment building. It's not the real McCoy. There are tables and chairs down there, there is also a fountain and a Jacuzzi. When we first moved into the building, we doubted we would use either the garden or the heated spa. The first seemed too communal. Who wants to carry all their food down in an elevator and out the back door to a shared garden? The latter seemed too *Three's Company.* Who wants to put on a swimsuit, descend once again down the public elevator, and soak in a hot tub and risk sharing bubbles with a heavily medallioned swinging Larry? Finally, we gave in. So what if the neighbors on the third floor see us on the elevator in our swim clothes? So what if we have to carry pitchers and serving plates and napkins and all the like down the elevator and through the lobby? As it turns out, we are always alone in the garden and alone in the Jacuzzi. Other tenants' sense of trepidation has in fact served us very well. Tonight, in the garden, Jason served a roasted pork tenderloin salad. It was an amazing mixture of everything bad (the pork, the brown sugar in the dressing) and everything good (fresh spinach, cabbage, golden raisins, sections of orange, avocado). It was wonderful, but I'm greedy. I want more. I long for a tableau out of Seurat's *A Sunday Afternoon on the Island of La Grande Jatte.* I want green spaces and a blanket and a basket full of exquisite food (I'll take those thirty dishes, Mrs. Beeton), and if I can be picky, since it's my dream, I want a nearby body of water to wade in. A lake would be perfect. A river would do.

~

"Life itself is the proper binge," Julia Child said. My mother, who is not Julia Child, used to tell me that the problem in my life is too many choices. She would say, "If you had two frocks, a red frock and a blue frock, then you would simply wear the one you hadn't worn the day before." My mother-in-law has also said that while being a stay-at-home mom was not a perfect life, she does not envy my generation's quest to have it all. Sometimes I wonder how to balance all the wants. When I was little, I wanted everything just once. I wanted to see Paris, just once. I wanted the boy I had a crush on to kiss me, just once. I wanted God to help me pass the test I didn't study for, just once. Now that I'm older, my desires aren't so simple. Going to Paris only made me want to go again and again. Running a ten-mile race made me want to run more races, which means more training. A fun dinner party makes me want to throw more dinner parties, which means more grocery shopping and more time cooking and cleaning and everything else. How to feed all those desires? How to satiate so much greed? Just for today, decide one way in which you can be absolutely spendthrift: talk on the phone with a dear friend until the cradle makes your ear wet and you don't have a thing to say; hop in a bathtub with a small bottle of bubbles and blow bubbles until your skin is like a prune; and if you are feeling peckish, save up all the calories you are counting, pick one day to cheat, and make yourself a perfect picnic—even if it's pouring outside and you have to serve it on your living room floor.

It is purely subjective, but the menu that follows is my definition of the proper binge.

∾

SOFT-SHELL CRABS

2 SERVINGS

¼ cup flour

½ tablespoon Old Bay seasoning

2 teaspoons salt

2 teaspoons freshly ground black pepper

3 tablespoons olive oil

4 soft-shell crabs, clipped and cleaned

Heat an iron skillet, over high heat until warm. Mix together the flour, Old Bay seasoning, salt, and pepper. Pour the olive oil into the heated skillet and wait until you see the first glimpse of smoke rising from its surface. Dredge the crabs in the flour mixture and drop them into the hot oil. Flip the crabs over after 1½ minutes and turn the skillet 180 degrees. After another 1½ minutes, remove the crabs from the skillet and place them on paper towels to drain off the excess oil. Serve immediately.

∽

SOUR CREAM-CHIVE DIP WITH GOURMET
LOW-FAT POTATO CHIPS

2 SERVINGS

¾ cup low-fat sour cream (do not substitute fat-free)

3 ounces soft goat cheese, crumbled

1 shallot, minced

Juice of 1 large lemon

Small handful of fresh chives, chopped

1 teaspoon sea salt

Large bag low-fat salt and pepper potato chips

> Mix all the ingredients except the chips together in a bowl, making sure the goat cheese is blended with the sour cream. Cover and chill the dip for at least 1½ hours before serving with the potato chips.

∽

CUPCAKES WITH BUTTERCREAM ICING

24 CUPCAKES

FOR THE CUPCAKES

1 cup (2 sticks) unsalted butter, softened

2 cups sugar

4 large eggs, at room temperature

1½ cups self-rising flour

1¼ cups all-purpose flour

1 cup milk

1 teaspoon vanilla extract

FOR THE ICING

1 cup (2 sticks) unsalted butter, softened

8 cups confectioners' sugar, sifted

½ cup milk

2 teaspoons vanilla extract

Food coloring, optional

Preheat the oven to 350°F. Line two 12-cup medium muffin tins with cupcake papers.

In a large bowl, using the medium speed of an electric mixer, cream the butter until smooth. Add the sugar gradually and beat until fluffy, about 3 minutes. Add the eggs one at a time, beating well after each addition. Combine the flours and add in four parts, alternating with the milk and vanilla extract, beating well after each addition.

Spoon the batter into the muffin cups to about three-quarters full. Bake for 20 to 22 minutes, until the tops spring back when lightly touched. Remove the cupcakes from pans and cool completely on a rack before icing.

For the icing, place the butter in a large mixing bowl. Add 4 cups of the sugar, then the milk and the vanilla extract. Beat until smooth and creamy. Gradually add the remaining sugar, 1 cup at a time, until the icing is a good spreading consistency. If you want to add a few drops of food coloring, now's the time. Use and store the icing at room temperature, as icing will set if chilled. It keeps well in an airtight container for 3 days.

Serve this entire meal with champagne. My choice would be Sofia Blanc de Blanc, which comes in an adorable tiny little can and a matching straw. *Bon appetit!*

A Word or Two or Three about Rejection

and the Importance of Fighting for Your Joy

OFTEN THINK THAT I'VE CHOSEN THE WORST profession for my particular temperament. Given that I can't bear rejection, I've chosen a field where rejection is an imminent, permanent part of my job. Among the writing projects I do for magazines, books, television, and film, I think it's safe to say that I average about a half dozen rejections a month. Though there are seasons—a script making the rounds, a magazine pitch that goes out and comes back and goes out again—when there may be a rejection every single day of the week. Case in point, a recent conversation that I had with an editor at a national women's magazine. I had a friendly rapport with the editor-in-chief, who expressed admiration for my work and encouraged me to submit ideas, or "pitches," to use the magazine parlance, for her monthly. She set me up with a senior editor who would shepherd my ideas and for months, it seemed like the blind date from hell that wouldn't end. I would call and suggest an article about hiking or buying your first house or breaking up with a friend. The editor would say no, but why don't you try something else. After about six tries, the editor called me up to say, "I don't really like your writing. I know you are well published, but I don't see what all the hoopla is about. I'm only talking to you because my boss asked me to. But clearly, the quality of ideas you've sent shows that I was right and she was wrong. You're not a right fit for this magazine." I held the phone away from my ear, hoping against hope that some of what was coming through might ooze down the handle and not land, Nickelodeon style, like green slime all over my face. Then I said, "How about this?" One more pitch, one more chance to prove that I was good enough and that I could do this. The editor paused for what seemed like an eternity, and said, "Okay, why don't you try that? I mean if you could write it down in an interesting way, and not a boring way, like your other ideas, that could be good." I hung up the phone, still feeling the sting. I had won the first round. There was an assignment in the works, a contract was on its way to my house. But I was clearly not out of the woods: if I could write it down? Yes, of course, I was a writer. "In an interesting way, not a boring way, like your other ideas." Oh, dear.

As it was, that particular piece bumped along for months. Every phone call was an indignation about my appalling lack of talent. Every revise met with disappointment and disgust. Until the editor called to say that she was "putting the piece out of its misery." For weeks, I deliberated about what to do with the kill fee from the piece—when a magazine "kills" an article that they've assigned, they are required to pay you 25 percent of the fee, hence the term. It's a funny term, *kill fee*. Because it certainly feels like you've been stabbed when an editor calls to say that she is not accepting the article and she is paying you only 25 percent of what you had been promised. As the months went by, I began to figure out that the money from this article was not going to suit its original purposes. My July mortgage came and went, I found another way to keep a roof over my head. Plane tickets to go home for the holidays were purchased by other means. Then, when finally the kill fee was processed, it seemed that using the money responsibly was not what I should do. I decided that the check for roughly $400 should be spent frivolously, and during the weeks I awaited its arrival, I made a hundred plans for my kill fee. Should I go to Kinara, my favorite spa in Los Angeles and treat myself to a day of beauty? There was a package that I long dreamed of doing called "the Uptown Girl"; it consisted of a Cleopatra milk bath, a custom massage, a red carpet facial, lunch in the spa restaurant, and champagne all day long. Then a funny thing happened: I spent so much time on the Kinara Web site that by the time the kill fee arrived, I almost felt like I'd already done the Uptown Girl package. I'd fantasized about it so much, I had actually kind of enjoyed it already. So I put the money aside in what I call my "art fund" to buy the paintings and photographs that I have begun to collect, little by little. These days, I am dreaming of a new Elina Brotherus photograph. I already have two, but I am longing for a third. It is called "Model Study 7," and it is like a Vermeer come to life. This is no accident, as Elina calls her photographs "the new painting." I look forward to buying the Elina photograph because I know that it will be more than a balm for the rejection I have endured. It reminds me of an interview I once read with Michael Caine. The journalist was giving him a hard time about a movie he made, a movie that the critics had decimated. Michael Caine said, sanguinely, "I have never seen the film, . . . but I have seen the house that it built, and it is terrific."

Whatever I do with my kill fee, I know that I will enjoy it. Because this is the thing about rejection, it is never useless. There are always spoils. My friend's mother, Valentine Hill, used to tell her daughter, "Sometimes you disqualify yourself even before the game begins. You have to do your best and let God do the rest." I remember once I was in the process of being rejected by a very powerful New York editor. I went to have my eyebrows tweezed for the first time. Lying in the back room of a nail salon while hair by hair was plucked out of my eyebrow by a woman who missed her calling as a torturer in the Middle Ages. And what I remember thinking was no matter what this woman did to me professionally, she was not going to strap me to a table and pull every hair out of my eyebrow. There is heartbreak and there is physical pain. And for the most part, when you go for it, when you put yourself out there and chase your dreams, you may get your heart broken, but no one's going to actually wield sticks and stones.

⌒

Years ago, when I was on a quest for a spiritual home, I found myself at a service of the First Presbyterian Church of Brooklyn. I had stayed away from this beautiful nineteenth-century masterpiece because of the sign on the outside that said something like "We are a multiracial congregation looking toward the future." It felt a little too "We Are the World" for me, but it was a beautiful church and geographically desirable, a short ten-minute walk from my house. Service was at eleven A.M., which seemed a reasonable bargain to strike with God during a time when I regularly slept until noon. So I went to the service, and while the choir left a lot to be desired, I was mesmerized by the pastor, Dr. Paul Smith. He was smart, down to earth, deeply spiritual, but no Bible thumper. And one of the first sermons that I heard Dr. Smith give was titled "A Delay Is Not a Denial." I had never heard this phrase before, and given my precarious professional and romantic life at the time, the saying and the sermon really hit home for me. I began to believe that just because my work was being rejected left and right, just because I was having no luck at all meeting a man, it didn't mean that it wouldn't happen for me eventually.

When I was growing up, my mother had tried hard to communicate the same notion to me, but the words she used were very different. What my mother said was "Patience is a virtue." So when I was impatient, not only did I feel rejected, poor in my work prospects, and poor in love, but I could also add to the list of troubles that I was sorely lacking in the virtue of patience. Dr. Smith's words, on the other hand, seemed to be tinged with hope: A delay is not a denial. God is not laughing in your face. Keep hope alive.

So it was that the way I dealt with rejection began to shift ever so slightly. I started to give myself a three-day mourning process for dealing with the sadness of a magazine turning me down or a guy I liked giving me the heave-ho. On the first day, I could cry as much as I wanted. On the second day, I could cry, but I had to get out of the house. On the third day, I could cry, but I had to do something to get back on the horse: send out another magazine pitch or dress up cute and go out to a bar with my girlfriends or, better yet, with one of my walkers, the coterie of guy friends who always made me feel charming and beautiful. For the most part, this is a process I keep up to this day, and I am very lucky to now be married to a man who does a very good job of making me feel charming and beautiful even when all evidence indicates otherwise.

And over the years, time has proven that it is indeed true, that a delay is not a denial. Article ideas that are rejected at a dozen places eventually find a happy home. The fact that I am writing this book is evidence that, as the gospel song says, even after the darkest night, dawn comes. After being rejected by who knows how many men in the greater New York area, I met my husband who not only fell in love with me but put the pedal to the metal and proposed within a shocking eight months of our first date. After spending years in what felt like my own romantic version of the movie *The Terminal*, I met my husband and I discovered that Dr. Smith had been more than right. God wasn't holding out on me, a delay isn't a denial.

Of course, I had to do my part. If you haven't read Patti LaBelle's book *Don't Block the Blessings*, I seriously recommend that you do. Even if you are a person who cares nothing for religion, I suggest you pick it up because it isn't so much about God as it is about getting out of your own way. I also recommend the audio version because Patti's speaking voice is just as magical as her singing voice. I listened to *Don't Block the Blessings* in the car, I listened to it in the kitchen while I cooked, I listened to it in bed through a little tape recorder that I kept on my nightstand. I listened to it until what my dear friend Retha Powers once described as "head knowledge" became "heart knowledge." And slowly but surely, I put those words to practice in my life. I learned that while I may dream about being a writer for XYZ magazine, I had to stop blocking the blessings and recognize the opportunities that were there for me at ABC magazine. Once while dating a man who treated me so poorly that the twists and turns in our relationship were beginning to resemble a soap opera plot line, I realized that I had to break it off with him. I had loved him, and when it was good, it was so very, very good; but I listened to Patti and I realized that this man was blocking my blessings. What if we were at a party and the man who would love me the way I longed to be loved were there? He would see me with my fella, looking happy as all get out as we always did in public, and he would never approach me. I needed to learn to let go of good (or, in this case, fair to partly cloudy) to make room for great.

It was in this place, this process of not blocking my blessings, that I learned that life is just about steeling yourself against rejection. I was only halfway there when I learned to make myself strong enough (that three-day rule) not to fall apart every time the world told me no. The other half of the equation was setting the table for joy. It was about going where the love was, professionally. It was about clearing a place in my head and my heart for the people and opportunities that I desired. My husband likes to make fun of the whole "If you can conceive it, you can receive it" mind-set. He says this encourages the most trifling behavior: people who pray for good parking spaces and 50 percent off cashmere at Barney's. But I know that while I have sometimes been given bigger things, greater experiences than I could imagine, every good thing in my life began with a small prayer, a step forward toward joy.

Once, after a wretched breakup, I took a business trip

to Spain. On the plane, I made a list of the twelve most important qualities to me in a man. I did it on a plane because, silly as it seems, I looked out at the sky and I felt closer to Heaven. When I returned from the trip, my husband called and asked me out on a date. At first, I thought he wouldn't last longer than the milk in my fridge, a nice guy, but. . . . Yet each date revealed that he possessed a quality that I had written on that list, until I began to believe that I had fallen into a deep delusion, where I'd made up this man, like a child conjures an imaginary friend.

Another time, I stuck a note on my bulletin board, "I want to see the world." Periodically, I would take it down and write it in different ways on different colored pieces of paper. About six months later, I was organizing the board, and seriously considering throwing the piece of paper away, when I received a call from *Travel + Leisure* magazine: Did I want to test-drive a convertible in Baja and write about it? They would pay all of my expenses, and I could bring a friend. I kissed the piece of paper and thanked my lucky stars.

Years ago, my friend, the novelist and playwright Shay Youngblood, gave me a Tibetan wishing bowl. The present, which I believe she purchased at a museum, arrived unexpectedly on a day that was not my birthday and was not Christmas. Shay is the most amazing friend in this way. We see each other only a few times a year, but she has a way of popping up in my life just when I need a boost of the joy she provides: A card arrives on the same day when I get a rejection letter for a grant I was confident that I would receive. I get a phone message from Shay, the minute I walk in the door after nearly being run off the road by some crazy driver. I open the front door, my hands still shaking from the close call, and there is Shay's voice, melodic and teeming with life, like a cradle to catch my fall.

The day that Shay gave me the Tibetan wishing bowl, she suggested that I write down my heart's desires and put them in the bowl. Then, quoting an African proverb, she gave me the ultimate Shay-ism. She said, "Move your feet when you pray." My friend Lise Funderburg has a variation on this, she calls it the Lotto motto, quoting the slogan of the New York State lottery system, she says, "You've got to be in it to win it." And so I try, I try to be in it.

I once read an article in which financial guru Suze Orman said that when you are feeling poor, write a check to a good cause. Even if the check is as small as five dollars, the pure act of giving opens you up for more. I have done this for years now and found that it is true. When I am at my financial wits end, I write a check and money appears. Someone accepts an article that I wrote and calls to say the check is in the mail. A friend gives me a gift certificate for a massage to thank me for a favor I had long forgotten. I can't use the gift certificate to pay my electric bill, but it is the respite I need during a tough time. Having had so much success with the financial circle of life, I have in recent years, begun to search out luck when I need it. When I am feeling unlucky, I enter a sweepstakes or I buy a raffle ticket. Raffles aren't always available, but it is easy enough to find a free sweepstakes online, my favorite sites to troll are www.self.com, www.lifetimetv.com, and www.style.com. I haven't actually won anything from these particular sites, but the forward motion of finding luck when you are looking for it has proven itself to me again and again.

Case in point: About three months ago, I was going through a rough patch. Nothing was severely wrong, it was just that nothing was spectacularly right. So hoping to pull myself out of my doldrums, I went on www.epicurious.com/gourmet/ because they have the best sweepstakes and they are all related to food. They were running a sweepstakes to win a *Gourmet* trip to London. I decided to enter. (Almost all of these sweepstakes are related to subscriptions, but you can click on "no purchase necessary" and enter for free.) The grand prize winner and their lucky guest got a free ticket to London, four nights in a swank hotel, and dinner at a top restaurant. I entered and instantly felt better about my day, having moved away from my feelings of utter worthlessness and segued into a deeply fulfilling fantasy of an all-expenses-paid getaway to London. A few weeks later, I got a phone call from our friend Gretchen Connelly. Her husband, Chris, is a host on ABC and attends the Oscars every year. In Chris's Oscar basket, there was a gift certificate for dinner for twelve, catered at your house, by Wolfgang Puck. It was Chris's birthday, the gift certificate was about to expire, Gretchen wanted to know if she could have the dinner catered at our house. A few weeks later, six tuxedoed members of Wolfgang's Puck staff, took over our kitchen, complete with walkie-talkies like Secret Service men in the movies. They brought wine, steaks, and dozens of pots and pans of heartbreakingly delicious food. Jason and I let them in, and changed into something chic. An hour later, Chris and Gretchen arrived with their friends and family. For two hours, we had the most sophisticated cocktail party in our living room, waiters sailed in and out, wordlessly, refilling wineglasses and serving delectable appetizers: mini cheeseburgers, sashimi in tiny little ice cream cones, and the best damned fried oysters I have ever had in my life. Then we were led into the dining room, where we were gifted—there is no other word—with the most amazing four-course meal. Then the staff of four—who has staff these days?—cleaned it all up and left our kitchen more spotless than they had found it. Did I mention we ate Wolfgang Puck leftovers for days? I hadn't won the *Gourmet* sweepstakes, but in a way I had. And I can't help but feel that it all started the moment I decided to shake the mean reds by trolling for a bit of luck online.

Setting the Table for Joy

T IS NOT THE SEXIEST OF FOODS, BUT I LOVE SOUP. I love it with a passion that other more sophisticated women save for oysters and caviar and foie gras. We map the cities we love with landmarks: our favorite shops, schools we once attended, the addresses of men we once loved. For me, New York is a cauldron of soup. If I am in Soho, then I go to Kelly and Ping for big bowls of Asian noodle soup that remind me of the time I spent in Japan—big udon noodles, bright pink pieces of pork, and an almost immodest amount of flavor for the clear broth that soup maintains. It as if all spices were rendered invisible in the hot cloudy water. If I am near Union Square, I visit Gramercy Tavern. Midtown, I go to Menchanko Tei. In the summer, the tavern serves gazpacho and in the winter, a tomato and garlic bread soup that makes me moan like Meg Ryan in *When Harry Met Sally.* Just north of Times Square, there is Victor's, the famous Cuban restaurant, which serves many delectable dishes; but I won't taste a single *plantano* or a bite of *ropa vieja* until I have a bowl of their black bean soup.

Farther uptown and farther downtown, there are more delights: bowl upon bowl of soup. In my mind, they pile up and I carry them around, expertly, like a carnival performer juggling plates. But as much as I love eating soup, what I love most is making it. Soup is the ultimate party food. You make filet mignon and when a dinner guest shows up with unexpected guests, there is panic; and depending on your temperament, there is embarrassment and rudeness. Salmon is the universal fancy food in this age of healthy eating, but a salmon steak divided does not make a pretty plate, and extra rations aren't always easily ordered up.

There is always enough with soup. And I know this, in part, because I grew up in a Panamanian household where my mother often made a rich chicken soup, flavored with unattractive bones and scraps and Sazón Goya, a spice that in our house is as essential as air. She sent us with soup to friends who lived nearby, and when there were unexpected visitors, whatever we were having for dinner—chicken, fish, beef—was quickly turned into soup.

Growing up with an immigrant parent provides many moments of comic relief, but this is one of my favorites. One day I was in the kitchen, and my mother was singing along to Aretha Franklin. Aretha said, "What you want?" And my mother sang, "Soup!" Aretha said, "Baby, I got it." And my mother said, "Soup!" I stopped her and asked, "What are you talking about? The chorus is 'ooo' " She said, "No, it's not. It's soup. You respect somebody and you give them soup. A man comes home from work and his wife says, 'What you want?' And he says, 'Soup.' His wife tells him, "Baby I got it—'soup.' " I shook my head no. "That's not what the song says." My mother shrugged. "Well, that's how it makes sense to me." And now that I am married and older, it sort of makes sense to me, too. My husband loves my soup. The type varies. These days, it is an African peanut soup, inspired by a roommate I once had from the Ivory Coast, and is made, incredibly, with two heaping tablespoons of peanut butter.

Perhaps I love soup because at the heart of it is a meal of transformation. A broth is either thickened or made thin (by straining out the denser elements). A pot of soup is the Statue of Liberty of food, it finds a place for everything that comes to its shores. Dingy vegetables, fish and meat bones contribute their paltry offerings to the stock. There is room in soup for pasta and rice and just about anything you can think of. The first cookbook published in America (a 1742 edition of E. Smith's *The Compleat Housewife*) included a bounty of soup recipes whose names reflect Colonial spelling: Soop Sante, Pease Soop, Craw Fish Soop, Broothe and Green Pease Soup. Although fruit soups are just beginning to gain in popularity here, in China they are often served as a medicinal kind of dessert. Banana and strawberry soups have a cooling effect and are believed to fight infection. Other fruit soups, litchee and guava in particular, have a warming effect. The business of making soup is essentially a practice of alchemy, the whole is always, if not greater than, then different from, livelier than the sum of its parts. And isn't that what we want to believe about ourselves, that despite the fact that we are just skin and bones and so very human, that we are also *more*?

I have a philosophy about creating mouth-watering meals: I double the most delicious ingredient in the recipe. When I make my friend Louise's sauerbraten recipe: a pot roast with a ginger gravy, I make the gravy with ginger snaps and I double the amount of ginger snaps so that the gravy is rich and sweet. I am far from a spectacular cook, but I am a generous one. It is sometimes hard to be giving in life—to cut an annoying co-worker some slack or to find the patience for a friend who constantly needs a shoulder to cry on. But I have found that generosity in the kitchen is good practice for generosity in life.

I do not know the cooks at Le Pain Quotidien in Los Angeles. But I believe they know a great deal about generosity. Gazpacho, the cold tomato soup that originated in Spain, is a simple soup that can be ruined in a hundred different ways. A sloppy gazpacho can taste like a cold spicy ketchup or a watered down Bloody Mary or a bowl of runny tomatoes. But the gazpacho at Le Pain Quotidien is thick, but never mealy. Every slurp and mouthful is full of flavor and spice and surprise—a julienne of cucumber, a spoonful of basil purée. You never get the feeling that the cook is scraping the bottom, each bowl feels like the first bowl out of the pot: chock-full of good stuff.

Soup is magic. And not only because it is my culinary go-to food. My earliest memory of going to school was of being in kindergarten and hearing the story of Stone Soup. Briefly told, there is a peddler—perhaps he is wandering through Eastern Europe, Africa, or Asia. It is a time of great famine. He asks for a room for the night but is told to move on. The village he has happened on is starving. There is no room to spare, there is no food. What a shame, he tells the villagers, because he was yearning to cook up a pot of his magical stone soup. He sets up a cauldron and a pot of water and begins to boil his magic stone. Curiosity grows. "Stone soup is good," he muses aloud, "but it is even better with cabbage." And a bit of cabbage appears. "Stone soup with cabbage is delicious," he reminisces. "But once I had stone soup with cabbage and salt beef and that was really something!" The village butcher manages to rustle up a piece of salt beef. And so on and so forth with carrots, potatoes, onions, mushrooms until the soup was finished and the entire village partook in the feast. The villagers offered the peddler all the gold they had for that magic stone, but he turned them down. The next day, he was gone. But for years afterward, he was remembered as making the best soup anyone had ever had.

My mother's lessons about religion veered from the superstitious (don't put your purse on the floor, lest you lose all your money) to the philosophical (those who believe in nothing are dangerous and capable of anything.) But what I remember most, what I try to carry with me every day, is that the shortest prayer in the world is thank you. My mother taught us that the easiest way to show God how grateful we were for whatever little we had, was to share. In our family, the tradition of sharing was rooted at the dinner table.

This legacy of gratitude actually began with my

grandmother Flora, who raised five children in a one-room apartment in Colón, Panama. My grandmother worked in the Canal laundry, and money was always tight. Nevertheless, she had an uncanny awareness of who was in need: which woman had lost her job, whose husband had left her the week before. On Sunday nights when she cooked, she always prepared a plate for a neighbor. She sent my mother and her siblings as her emissaries, believing that charity is more acceptable when it comes from children. Even if the neighbor in need was someone my grandmother would not exchange two words with on the street, she sent a plate. "Take this to Señora So and So," were her stern orders. "Bring the dish back." My mother remembers that as a child, she grew to hate natural disasters, because my grandmother took the radio reports as personal telegrams for help. "If we had two pairs of shoes," my mother tells me, "and there was a hurricane, one pair would be sent to the Red Cross."

As a child, my mother found my grandmother's generosity puzzling. But as an adult, she walked the walk. In our Brooklyn apartment, she lamented that the concrete walls were too thick for the kind of chairty she'd been raised on. In Panama, she said, if you didn't smell anything cooking from the neighbor next door, you knew to send something—anything. Still, I remember my mother making plates for other Panamanians in the building: the bachelor on the second floor, the elderly woman down the hall. Even when there was so little food that my brother and I greedily counted the pieces of chicken in the arroz con pollo, my mother repeated the biblical miracle of loaves and fishes every Sunday night, making whatever we had stretch. I learned that when you share what you have there is always enough. "*Para compartir es una bendición*," my mother said. And I learned that to share, especially food, is both an act of gratitude and an act of faith. If you share today, tomorrow there will be more.

In my own life, I try to make cooking for friends a similar sort of blessing. Even when I lived alone, I would make big pots of soup and leave messages for friends: Come over, and if you can't stay, take a Tupperware container of food to go. Because of my Panamanian heritage, I shudder at the idea of throwing a party where the only thing my guests have to dine on is potato chips and beer. I once planned a dinner party on a Saturday, but the night before I had to work late. The following morning, I woke up at noon, having walked through the door only seven hours before. The phone rang: It was my mother. "What are you serving for dinner?" she asked. "I have no idea," I told her, groggily. My mother, industrious, worried, and a thousand miles away in Miami would not be deterred. "You could serve *bacalao* (codfish), but there's no time to soak the fish." I told her I would think about it and call her back. An hour later, the phone rang, it was my favorite aunt, Aunt Diana. "I hear you worked late and are having people over," my aunt said. "What are you going to do?" I gave her the same answer, I didn't know. "Maybe I'll order in a pizza," I said, only half-joking. My aunt shuddered, audibly. "Ay, *niña*, you know we don't do things like *that*!" she said, as if I'd suggested that I would parade down Fifth Avenue in nothing but my undies and a pair of sunglasses. "Maybe you should go to El Viejo Yayo," she suggested, naming a favorite local Latin restaurant. "Pick up some rice with black beans and roasted chicken. That would be nice."

In the end, I relied on an oldie but goodie. A Tahitian crabmeat soup, that my friends like to refer to as "a bucket of sin." The ingredients are simple, but luxurious: fresh crabmeat, coconut milk, butter, and spinach. I am not a fan of cream soups, but the coconut milk blends so seamlessly with the crabmeat in this recipe. I am a big fan of spices. I never met a marinade I didn't like, and I'm loath to cook a piece of chicken or beef or fish if I have not seasoned it with my favorite spices first. But the crabmeat soup calls for only two spices: salt and pepper. And although I have experimented: a toss of paprika here, a dash of curry there, the fact is that the soup tastes best with the spices that are called for: salt and pepper.

Although I was exhausted from working late the

night before, I cleared my mind of such thoughts as I poured each ingredient into the pot. I imagined myself as the temptress chef in *Like Water for Chocolate*; and as I stirred the soup, I thanked God for all of my blessings, prayed that my dinner party would be a blessing for each person who walked through the door. Thanksgiving is an amazing holiday, I told myself on that January afternoon. Especially when you try to celebrate it every day.

It is a cliché, the whole "chicken soup for the soul" thing. But I would be remiss if I did not talk about the healing properties of soup. When I was first dating my husband, I got a terrible cold, and he left me a strange, albeit charming, message about the "handsome man soup delivery service." At the time, I feared that this message, long, rambling, and disjointed, might be a deal breaker. Who said he was handsome? I wanted to know. Who said I wanted him to bring me soup? I wondered. But as it was, I was able to take the message in the spirit it was intended. He did not know me well, but he wanted to take care of me. And months later, when he proposed, this was the foundation on which I knew our marriage would be built. He knew me well. He wanted to take care of me. He might not always succeed, but he would always do his best.

Recently, I ran into an old friend who brought up soup in quite a different context. Last year, I'd had an infection in my breast, which combined with a tumor, had required surgery. As my grandmother had died of breast cancer, this scare had been particularly frightening for me. I had not seen my friend during this time. "I heard you were sick," she said. "I'm glad you're okay." I nodded my head and tried to change the subject. It was and is still not my favorite topic. "I'm sorry I never called," my friend said. "It's just that I know how I am. I would've flown into Florence Nightingale mode, and I would've been over there every two seconds, cleaning your house and making you soup." I assured her that it was okay. But as the weeks go by, something about her comments still sting. I understand avoiding the trap of overgiving, but I can't help but wonder. Isn't there some middle ground between the complete silence I felt during my illness and the pendulum swing of being at my house every day, cleaning and making soup?

If I am honest, I can work myself up into quite a frenzy about how horrible the months of being sick were. I think of how I felt, the first night my husband took me to the emergency room when my breasts started leaking. I could not explain the strange discharge in my breasts or why I had to peel my shirt off of my chest. I remember thinking that God was punishing me for waiting too long to have children. "The Big Guy is saying, 'You're wasting both your ovaries and my time.' " I told my husband, "Homey don't play that." Then there was the ultrasound, followed by the mammogram, followed by the second ultrasound. The day of my mammogram, I was so scared. But I'd had an extended illness a few years before, a hernia surgery with a medley of complications followed by an extended bout of mono. I found myself reaching for the phone to call a friend to go to the doctor's with me or to come out to lunch and cry, and I held back. Better not call her, I told myself. You used your sick chits with her on the hernia. Better not call him, I told myself. He took you to the doctor a lot the last time. Unlike the last time I was sick, this time around I had my husband to hold my hand and make me food and give me a bath and change my bandages. But I missed my friends, and I noticed what felt like conspicuous silences. Maybe I'm mad at my friend, who admitted to staying away, not because of her failure as a friend but because of the way I battened down how much I needed her. Maybe she was right. Maybe soup was at the center of it, after all. I wanted her to make stone soup with me. But I did not have the courage to set the water a boiling and put my own stone in the pot.

I am afraid to be vulnerable. In college, I kept a running list of stupid things that I had said that day. In junior high school, I remember keeping a similar list of girls who hated me. Growing up in the 1970s and early 1980s, the literature that changed my life were powerful meditations on women and friendship: *The Color Purple, Women of Brewster*

Place, Sula. These books taught me that women create women in every sense that matters, that one woman can save another woman's life and that, conversely, a woman can slay another woman without laying a finger on her. These literary renderings made real on paper what I had already experienced. I am seven, I am nine, I am eleven, and there is a girl—always one who is the ringleader— and maybe she has minions. But there is a girl, at least one, and she rules my world. Sometimes she has red hair and an impossible smattering of freckles that seem more like something off of television than like a girl walking down our ordinary Brooklyn street. Sometimes she is tall, taller than anyone in our grade. Sometimes she is as dark as Cicely Tyson and sometimes her skin is the color of cinnamon, paprika, or dry mustard. She is always beautiful, she is always powerful; and even now, if I close my eyes and think of her, I can feel her breath on my neck when she whispered a secret or a command in my ear.

In my twenties, I valued the women in my life to the detriment of my romantic relationships with men. It was as if the "friend" in the word *boyfriend* was as silent and mysterious as the *e* at the end of certain words in French. I can remember nights when my mind ran wild with confusion and I felt so disconnected from the man sitting across the dinner table from me. My eyes shifted crazily to the clock above his head, wondering what excuse I might concoct to run to the store, meaning run to the payphone, so I could call a sister friend and speak until the words found a place of peace. The process of falling in love with my husband was built, for me, on a foundation of intimacy I never attempted before with men. When I felt the impulse to call a girlfriend, I called my husband and I tried, however awkward it felt, to speak freely. He has become my friend in the deepest sense of the word, and I consider this a badge of my growing maturity. Finally, I trust a man to be a friend in the way that I only trusted women before.

As a young woman, I sought out only female mentors: hungry for their attention, needy for their guidance. I was lucky. Many amazing women responded. I did not know then that mentorship did not consist of getting leagues of powerful women to sign up for free work on a project called Me. I was so selfish. I spent long valuable lunch hours and after-work drink meetings going on and on about myself. I tried to be appreciative: Thank God my mother had installed me with the thank-you note gene. But I was not always savvy enough, open enough, to say thank you to people who had touched my life in a substantial way. For a very long time, I regretted that. Then, recently, I had an experience that made me think more generously toward the girl that I once was. A girl that I mentor came to see me in my home office. She walked over to a book shelf and picked up a copy of *Sarah Phillips* by Andrea Lee. "Have you read this?" she asked. "I read it last summer. It's my favorite book in the world." I reminded her that I had actually given her *Sarah Phillips* as a present the Christmas before. I told her that I was glad it was her favorite book because it was one of my favorites as well. The look on her face held a hundred emotions: kinship, embarrassment, happiness, fear, confusion, and acceptance. I knew then that my former mentors, many of whom are still friends to this day, had seen the same layers of expression on my own young face. They had not judged me as I had judged myself. Perhaps because they knew that the kindness they had bestowed on me would eventually make its way to the next generation of women. "Oh yeah, that's right" my young friend finally said and as she settled into an armchair, we continued to talk, weaving a fabric of words and experience that have brought girls and women together for centuries.

A couple of years ago, I had the amazing pleasure of visiting Wheatleigh, a hotel in western Massachusetts that is two steps beyond posh. There was a fireplace in my room and a sweeping palazzo-style terrace. The bathroom, with its magnificent claw-foot tub and separate shower room, was almost the size of my entire New York apartment. That first night, my then fiancé and I had dinner in the hotel's more casual restaurant, the Library Bar. We sat in a small room filled with books, then opened yellowed volumes from the 1800s to read the menu that had been pasted inside. I knew what I would order, even before I asked the waiter to explain it. The menu read, "Soup, soup, soup, soup." As promised, the dish was four white demitasse cups, filled with soup, served on an exquisite white porcelain tray. There was a pumpkin soup and a split pea soup, a consommé, and a potato leek soup. I sipped each from its cup and it took all the discipline I had not to order four cups more. I was dizzy with satisfaction and the kind of fleeting excitement that comes when you know you are exactly where you have longed to be. Everything was perfection. Dinner had consisted of not one soup, but four. After months of practically sleeping at my office, I was in the country for an entire weekend with not a single thing to do. I would soon be married to the man I had waited a very long time to meet. The next day we went back to the Library Bar for lunch and I ordered the same thing. I said, "Soup, soup, soup, and soup." But what I was thinking was, "Love, love, love, and love."

∞

VERONICA'S FAMOUS CRABMEAT SOUP

4 SERVINGS

1 medium onion, diced

4 tablespoons butter

1 (13.5-ounce) can coconut cream

8 ounces heavy cream

8 ounces chicken stock

1 pound lump crabmeat

Salt and pepper, to taste

1 (10-ounce) package frozen chopped spinach

> In a large pot over heat, sauté the onion in the butter. Reduce the heat to medium low and add the remaining ingredients. Simmer for 30 minutes.

> Chef's DJ note: While cooking, listen to Betty Carter and Ray Charles's rendition of "Baby, It's Cold Outside."

PART II

Knocked Off Balance

A Girl's Guide to Staying on Her Feet

Everything You Need, You've Got

OW MUCH DO I LOVE THE BALLET? WHEN I WAS IN college, a woman I worked with invited me to go with her to see *The Nutcracker,* performed by the New York City Ballet. I went back every year, and the ballet has become a Christmas gift I give myself. One year, I went to see *The Harlem Nutcracker,* a modern-day variation on the classic by choreographer Donald Byrd and performed at the Brooklyn Academy of Music. Another year, my husband surprised me with a trip to Montreal. Fortune smiled on us as we managed to snag same-day tickets for the Canadian Ballet's performance of *Pique Dame* (The Queen of Spades). More recently, annual visits to Alvin Ailey's American Ballet Theater have replaced *The Nutcracker* as my tradition.

To watch dance and to actually dance, however, are worlds apart. I remember so distinctly taking ballet and tap as a little girl and the heartbreak when I realized we could not afford lessons anymore. It was the one time in my life when my extreme natural turnout was an asset. Now, it is only the occasional stranger who asks me if I once danced ballet. Most just look at me and remark that I walk like a duck. Ouch. Yet, the desire to dance ballet still lurks deep inside.

Years ago, I bought a ballet fitness tape. Ballet, the teacher promised, could help you gain strength and burn fat. This did not turn out to be true. I never broke a sweat, and I felt a little silly in my apartment, practicing my *pliés* and *grands jetés*. More recently, my local gym began offering a class in the New York City ballet technique. I figured that I could burn calories on the treadmill and tone in the ballet class.

I could hardly wait for my first ballet class. But when I arrived, I felt like I'd landed in that famous painting *Boulevard of Broken Dreams*. Our teacher, a former professional dancer, was beautiful, thin, dressed in a charcoal gray leotard and tights. The students ranged in age from twenty-five to fifty. There were about a dozen of us, and we were almost evenly decided in our sartorial choices. Half of the class was dressed like six-year-old would-be ballerinas: hair in chignons, pink leotards, pink tights, pink slippers. Forgive me for saying so, but this particular getup was flattering only on the teacher. And even she had chosen to go for the darker, more forgiving shade. The rest of us, dressed in our sweats and T-shirts, looked like linebackers. At least that's what I felt like as I spent the next fifty minutes going through the rudimentary techniques. All the ballet I had adored on stage seemed to slap me in the face with each *port de bras*, with every *ronde de jambe*. I looked in the mirror and all I could see was what I was not. At the end, our teacher promised, we would dance *Swan Lake*. And in the last ten minutes of the class, when the opening notes of that music I knew so well, lifted and carried us across the room, I was happy. My fellow students and I flashed each other silly grins. It was fun, but by the time I got home, the spell had worn off. And I wasn't anxious to take the class again.

The first time I took African dance was in every way the opposite. My teacher, Connie Bennett, had asked us to bring some sort of cloth wrap. We gathered that day, every shape and size, every color and age. I wore a sarong over my leggings and T-shirt. Other students wore similar wraps; still others simply tucked brightly colored Indonesian and African fabrics into their sweat pants and shorts. The music was lilting and rhythmic and we began to spread out across the room. Then Connie called the class to order and asked us to turn away from the mirror.

Funny thing about a group of smart, lively women: Following instructions is not our favorite thing. I could feel the energy in the room shift as people made comments underneath their breath, grumbled about the logic of it all. I, for one, wondered how I was supposed to follow the moves when I couldn't see what I was doing. Connie sensed our anxiety and made it clear that we were not there to follow her, but to dance with each other. There was no right way to do a step, she said, each body was different. It's a fact, Connie stated, that in African dance the bigger the better. "There is more power in every move," she said. We looked at each other as if to say, yeah right.

After the warm-up, the first dance that Connie taught us was called the Sowu. It is a West African dance that's typically taught to children. You trace the seven days of the week, alternating between the right and the left as your foot moves diagonally, like in the Charleston. With each step, we repeated after Connie:

Seven days a week, we honor our mommies and daddies.
Seven days a week, we honor our ancestors.
Seven days a week, we brush our teeth.
Seven days a week, we comb our hair.
Seven days a week, we try to be kind.

Connie encouraged us to fill in the blanks and so we did, calling out in unison.

Seven days a week, we eat ice cream.

Then at the end of the Sowu, we traced the days with our feet and we said:

Seven days a week, we do our best.
Seven days a week, we do our best.
Seven days a week, we do our best.

Repeating those words, over and over again was almost a religious experience for me. It was all I could do not to cry because I realized, as each word left my lips, that these were the truest words I had spoken in a very, very long time. "What an idiot," I tell myself when I make a simple mistake like leaving my work ID at home. "Loser," I call myself when I realize yet again that I have made a gross miscalculation in balancing my checkbook. The insults I can hurl at myself know no end. But the truth is seven days a week, I do my best. As I danced the Sowu and said those words, I was so grateful for the gift of kindness to myself.

"I have always depended on the kindness of strangers" is the famous line from *A Streetcar Named Desire*. What amazes me is how well we get by with so little kindness to ourselves. Of course, I see it more clearly in my friends than I do myself. It surprises me when I go to visit a busy mommy friend and she tells me that all she wants at the end of the day is to take a bubble bath. "Then why don't you do it?" I ask, maybe a little ignorantly. My friend rolls her eyes. "I don't have the time." We think what we want is a million dollars, a week at a luxury spa, a big house, a new job. What we really want, what makes a difference, are simple things, every day: a freshly made bed, a bubble bath, bread from our favorite bakery. There are so many days when I am driving home from work and I'll have a craving for the Chinese chicken salad from Trader Joe's. I would drive there for a houseguest. I would drive twice as far for a houseguest. But for myself? Excuses and more excuses.

Sometimes it seems that when it comes to being good to myself, my feet are blocks of solid stone. In the course of working on this chapter, the sun set. I looked across the room and thought, "It would be nice to light that candle." The only thing I love more than candles are flowers. But I would not get up and light the %&*$#@ candle. I looked at it and my first thought was, "I don't have time." Of course, it takes all of fifteen seconds to light a candle. My second thought was, "I don't know where the matches are." This was a bold-faced lie. I have, in recent months, actually established a drawer in the dining room where I keep the matches. So I got up, and I lit the candle. It seems like such a small thing, but I don't think it is. Aren't we all responsible for lighting the candles in our own lives?

～

I wish I could describe to you what the fifty minutes of Connie's African dance class are like. My fear is that the limitations of my language and experience will reduce something incredibly powerful to some New Age hokum. But since I insist on putting "writer" on my tax return, that means I must try to write even when words fail me. I've already told you that we face the windows, not the mirrors in the dance class. We begin with a warm-up, stretching it all out, and then we do the Sowu. Connie says something and we follow her in call-and-response fashion. Then for the next hour, Connie teaches us to do a harvest dance. We gather at one end of the room and we plant seeds, our bodies swaying low to the ground, as we travel in rows of a farmland we can see only in our minds. We "dance" back and forth that way: chopping our machetes through the bush, sorting the wheat from the chaff, reaching for fruit, carrying all we've gathered in our arms and skirts.

Connie tells us that although what we are doing are traditional harvest dances, we should "plant" and "sow" and "harvest" whatever it is that we want in our lives, outside of the classroom. She tells us that her life's philosophy is simple: "Move it or lose it. Movement is the way to stay juiced. If you're depressed, get moving. Broke? Get moving. Things will come to you." She suggests that when we dance the next go-round, we plant and sow and harvest something that is meaningful for us: good health, gold coins, Manolo Blahnik shoes, cashmere sweaters. I hear someone behind me whisper that she will be harvesting orgasms and everyone giggles again. The room practically crackles with anticipation. She has asked us to do more than dance, she has asked us to look into our own hearts, to flash a light on our own loves and lusts and longings. When we dance now, we are animated: We undulate our hips, we throw our arms forward and curl our fingers toward imaginary lovers, a few of us attempt small leaps instead of the safety of a simple lunge. I am one of the students who has begun to jump instead of step. In ballet, a large jump, a *grand jeté*, was dangerous. If this were ballet, I would be a leaping bovine. The mirror and all my bone-thin classmates would confirm this. But in African dance, there is no mirror. I am harvesting good health and champagne and chocolate. I am literally jumping for joy.

I was lucky enough to go to a college where everyone danced. The head of the dance department, Wendy Shifrin, is a glorious woman who manages to see beauty in every type of body and every type of movement. The college's annual dance concert is the community's equivalent of a county fair. You are liable to see anyone and everyone out there, doing their stuff. There are wheelchair dancers and three-hundred-pound dancers. There are ballet routines and jazz routines and routines choreographed to hip hop and reggae and bhangra. I was told by a friend that, in one recent performance, a quadriplegic student did a solo dance that stunned the auditorium into silence. And somewhere, in a galaxy far, far away, there is a videotape of me, doing a solo dance of my own choreography to a Prince song. This is not a good thing. Did I mention the dance involved props and a certain colored beret?

As embarrassed as I am by my own performance at

the college dance concert, I am grateful that I came of age in a place where I could think—for however short of time, however delusionally—of myself, as a dancer. Growing up in Brooklyn, my teenage years were a blur of parties where I spent the entire evening hugging the wall. I would tell myself that once the perfect song came on, I would get up and dance. If I actually did it, if I danced to just one song, I considered the party a huge success. Then I went to Simon's Rock and in every way that mattered, I decided that I didn't want to be the disco equivalent of a bench warmer. Sure, I suck. The rhythm and I have a major "on again, off again" relationship. But I love dancing. And so now—in no small part because of Wendy Shifrin and now, Connie—I dance.

I know that I am not the only person who has had a "come to Jesus" moment in Connie's class. I've seen the way women belly laugh in her class and I've seen women move slip slide from laughter right into tears. Connie says that we cry because we are learning to trust ourselves. "Any time you are working with your body, you are learning about trust and intuition," she says. "What happens is the crossing of the brain barrier. It's the dance drug. Sitting and reading just doesn't make the connection in the same way."

The first time Connie had students turn away from the mirror was purely accidental. She had come into the

studio to find that the mirrors were still covered with dec-
orations from the Christmas show. At first, she was bothered. Then she rolled with it and from the beginning, she
could see what a difference it makes for us, the students.
"African dance is about being able to move," Connie says.
"Not about judging yourself. Before, you would see the
students staring at themselves—no joy, no joy, and once
they stop looking in the mirror, *bam!*, they are completely
in their bodies. It's amazing to watch them let their inner
dancer move."

This is the other thing that I love about Connie.
She has an identical twin, Coko, who also teaches dance.
When I first met Connie, she would introduce herself and
explain about her twin. Now, a few years later, she tells
new students not to bother to try and tell her and Coko
apart. "Just call us 'Twin,' " she says. And everyone says,
no, I want to learn your name, I can do it. Then all week
long, during the course of the workshop, they proceed to
call her "Coko" and her sister, "Connie." "Just call me
'Twin,' " she says. "It's easy and I'm all about making life
easy. I want you to win." You know how people will tell
you to be careful of what you say because there are some
words you can't take back? Well, there are also some words
that, in their own accidental way, do a world of good. I can
tell you that there isn't a month that goes by that I don't
hear Connie's voice in my head when I come up against

some obstacle. And what she is saying, in the soundtrack of my brain, is "I want you to win."

~

I was deep into a Lifetime television marathon, when I came across a documentary about Marlo Thomas. It had been hours since I first sat down to watch "just one show." But day had turned to night, and I was beginning to feel way too close to Meredith Baxter Birney and Valerie Bertinelli, like "Maybe Valerie and Meredith would want to be my bridesmaids" close. I knew I needed to get on with the business of pretending to have a life when *Marlo Thomas, Intimate Portrait* came on. I have loved Marlo Thomas from *That Girl* to *Free to Be You and Me*. So I settled in to watch the show; and while I learned many things about Marlo Thomas that night, there is just one thing I will never forget. "Run your own race," Marlo said.

She may well have said, dance your own dance or sing your own song. It resonated for me because it seemed to me a perfectly succinct definition of what it means to live your life without comparing yourself to others. Run your own race. It turns out that this particular piece of advice was given to Marlo Thomas by her father, Danny Thomas. When she was making her stage debut, she was terrified of being compared to her famous father. He told her, "I raised you to be a Thoroughbred. When Thoroughbreds run they wear blinders to keep their eyes focused straight ahead with no distractions, no other horses. They hear the crowd but they don't listen. They just run their own race. That's what you have to do. Don't listen to anyone comparing you to me or to anyone else. You just run your own race." The next night, Thomas received a gift in her dressing room. It was a white box, with a red ribbon. Inside was a pair of horse blinders and a note that said, "Run your own race, Baby."

There's a dirty secret we women never want to admit. At least I never want to admit it. We envy other women. Even movie stars envy each other. Esther Williams, the million-dollar mermaid, once told a story about running into Ingrid Bergman in Paris. Williams said, "I envy you very much." Bergman's response was, "You envy me what? You had your own niche. Nobody's had what you've had." Williams said, "I know, I know, the wet swimmer. But your leading men . . ." Bergman, of course, had starred with Humphrey Bogart, Cary Grant, Gary Cooper. Bergman told Williams, "The reason you never had any of those leading men is because you didn't need them. You and your bathing suit in the water were co-stars enough."

Even we non—movie stars fantasize about each other's leading men. We also crave one another's bank accounts, wardrobes, and waistlines. The plethora of celebrity-oriented magazines and television shows might lead you to believe that we really want to be like someone famous, but the truth is that the women who get our goat are the women in our own lives. "How do we learn to covet?" Hannibal Lecter coos at FBI agent-in-training, Clarice Starling. "We covet what we see every day." Who's more threatening? Cindy Crawford, who in your mind lives on the pages of a glossy magazine, or the woman in your office, who is such a fox that your male boss stutters when she enters the room? Most of us don't ever believe that we could ever have Cindy's body, but when someone in our own world becomes the big winner, we do imagine that it could have been us.

Perfect example: My friend Risa is a biologist. When a young scientist won the top prize in Risa's field, she told me, "Not only is the woman talented but she's pretty. Scientists aren't supposed to be beautiful!" Months later a magazine ran a picture of the biologist—and the woman had put on a ton of weight. "I called a friend of mine and we just laughed," Risa told me. "I know. It's awful. But laughing made me feel better."

You might think that Risa is petty, vindictive, and so insecure that she would use others' weight problems to bolster her own ego. But Risa is one of the kindest people I know, and her reaction shows how deeply the roots of envy can reach within all of us.

Over the years, I've been both envied and the envier. And what I've discovered is that, first, pretending that envy doesn't exist won't make it go away. Second, when you stand up to your envy and look at it, without flinching, it can tell you powerful things about your own heart—what you want, what you must work harder to change—and what, ultimately, you've just got to let go.

To be jealous of someone is to feel a sense of competition: "She's smart, pretty, and thin—and I want to be smarter, prettier and thinner." Envy is even more insidious than jealousy. With envy, there's a sense not only that someone has something that you want but that by all rights that thing should be yours. People have asked me how I got a book deal or won a fellowship—and the tone in their voice is so accusing, you'd think I'd broken into their house in the middle of the night and stolen their success from underneath their pillow. Jealousy is a monster that quietly scratches at our hearts. But envy is that monster's Jurassic Park–dwelling cousin: a dinosaur that spews poisonous venom. We resent the envied and secretly wish her ill—and on top of that, we are embarrassed by the way we feel.

How do you put aside this kind of envy? Move on. I

simply won't allow myself to feel envious about some things. I'll never be six feet tall or have straight hair and green eyes. If I find myself envying someone because of her biology, I throw that sentiment right into a kind of mental waste bin labeled "Get Over It." I'm not saying that I don't have that initial pulse of envy coursing through my brain—I do. But this kind of envy is a waste of time.

It helps, too, to remind myself that there is nothing more alluring than the thrill of the unknown. Recently, I was having dinner with a producer friend of mine. He went on and on about this amazing writer that he was dying to work with. Had I ever met her? She was so smart. Her new script was so original. Throughout the meal, I could feel my heart breaking. I wanted my friend to be saying all of this stuff about me. Then I remembered, we had become friends because he had admired my work. If this is not giving myself too much credit, the reason I was having dinner with him is because once upon a time he had said all of those things—to a mutual friend—about me.

Too often, we hear compliments about another person like a bullhorn in church on a Sunday morning. By the same fashion, sometimes we do not hear compliments about ourselves at all. All throughout the dinner, my friend had been saying kind things about me. He marveled at my plans to run a race in Ojai and to go biking in Vietnam. He had praised my debut novel and my ideas for a screenplay. But I had barely heard any of those things at all. It wasn't until I turned off the blare of envy that I could settle in and enjoy dinner with my friend.

There's another reason that I sat up and paid attention when Marlo Thomas said, "Run your own race." That year, I had taken up running. I wasn't athletic by nature, or by nurture, but I felt there was something in running for *me*. I just did not know what. I could not run fast and I could not run distances. The runner's high that so many people talked about felt maddeningly elusive. I had always been a night owl, but running—at least for me and in New York City—was a morning activity. I knew there were women who ran at night, alone, but that didn't make me feel safe. So I gradually began to readjust my body clock. I read articles about how one became a morning person and while there were many good tips, the biggest one hit me like a ton of "no, duh" bricks: Go to bed earlier. In an attempt to cut down on the "think" time in the morning, I began to shower at night and go to sleep in my running clothes. That way when I woke up in the morning, there was one less thing to think about. My runs were never long: fifteen minutes at first, then twenty and thirty. I remember an ex-boyfriend saying to me, derisively, "Fifteen minutes isn't a run." I informed him that as long as I was running, it was actually a run. He rolled his eyes. "You're not a real runner. Maybe you should try something else."

Because I am goal oriented to a fault, all along, I believed that my morning runs were training. My idea was that I would do a 5k, then a 10k, then well, after that, I would see. I mentioned this to a co-worker, an art director named Lance Pettiford. He said, "Why not do the Army Ten Miler with me and my friends." Somehow, it never occurred to me that "No, thank you," was an option. Instead I said yes. With only two months to train and my longest run clocking in at three miles, I panicked. "You can always walk," Lance said. I agreed, but secretly hoped that it would not come to that. So I stepped up my training.

It was during this time that I began dating Jason. Playing it cool during dating had never been one of my strengths. When I fell for a guy, I fell hard. But Jason met me at a different point in my life. I was fresh off a rotten breakup. I was training for this race. I remember distinctly the afternoon he asked if he could come and see me and I told him only if he wanted to join me for a five-mile run. We ran and talked and when we came home, Jason made me the most exquisite Vietnamese roast chicken. When it came time for my race, Jason borrowed his parents' car to drive me from New York to Washington, D.C., where the race was going to be. The race was the day after his best friend's wedding, so he left right after the toasts. He drove me to Washington, and the morning of the race, he drove me to the starting line. I had no idea there would be so many people there. The runners numbered in the thousands; and within minutes, it was just me and a motley crew of stragglers.

For a few miles, I had jogged at a comfortable pace next to one particular woman. We did not talk, but we ran side by side. And I began to feel that if I could just keep pace with her, then I could do it. I could run the full ten miles. Then around mile three, she sped ahead. Of course, it was her right. She was running her own race. Then around mile four, I saw Jason. He was not holding a sign or hanging from a lamp post. He had not even been calling my name. If I had been looking in the other direction, I would have missed him. But I saw him and for the first time, maybe in my entire dating life, I knew what it meant to have someone waiting for me at the finish line.

In Connie Bennett's African dance class, we turn away from the mirror. She has taught me how to plant the seeds of my own desires and how to harvest them with leaps and turns and shimmies and shakes. I turn away from the mirror in her class and I do not need to see myself to feel beautiful. Meeting and marrying Jason has been another kind of dance, another way to reinvent my relationship to the mirror. Through him, I see a reflection of myself that my own heart is too self-critical to reflect. The challenge in our relationship is for me to accept it, to not turn away from the mirror of his love and respect and goodwill.

When I was a little girl, it seemed to me that the chances of my going to Hell were humungous, so I used to pray to God to help me be a good person. To be perfectly honest, I don't worry about that so much anymore. I give as much to others as I humanly can, in every way that I know how. I'm fairly confident that in the realm of fire and brimstone, I'm okay. My most secret prayer, of the last few years, is for God to help me stop beating myself up. I pray that I won't call myself names and that I won't get angry with myself over the littlest things. I know everybody has insecurities and everybody has days when they are down on themselves. But I'm talking about that kind of inward focused anger taken to the extreme. I pray that one day I will wake up and I will never again call myself "stupid" or "idiot" or "loser." Because it is my deepest belief that if I die tomorrow or forty years from now and I am still caught up in this self-critical bullshit then I will have missed it. A life spent beating myself up and telling myself off is like going to the World's Fair and spending the entire day in the Porta Potti. If not a colossal waste of time, then a very sad way to spend what could have been a marvelous day.

~

Like so many people, I knew very little about Beah Richards, except that she played Sidney Poitier's mother in the film *Guess Who's Coming to Dinner*. Then my friend Brandi sent out a group e-mail about Lisa Gay Hamilton's award-winning documentary, called *Beah: A Black Women Speaks*. I learned that Beah did not get her first paying acting job until she was thirty-six. Until then, Hamilton tells us she "sustains herself with poetry and activism." Although it took me nearly a month to watch the film after I had recorded it on TiVo, once I started watching it, I knew I would never forget it. Beah's words epitomize how I feel when I am in the joy place: when I am leaping across the room in an African dance class, when I am running around the yard with one of my nieces and nephews, when I am holding hands with my husband, walking to work. And it's her words that I want to remember when I am sitting in the courtroom of my internal judge who says that I am not organized enough, that I am not smart enough, that I am not and never will be enough. In the film, Beah gazed into the camera with the full force of her beauty and she said, "Being is mortal insistence in a complete and perfect state, lacking no essential characteristic. Everything you need, you got. Perfect. Maybe not yet realized, but perfect, complete."

The Hustle Award

WE WERE CLEANING OUT THE BASEMENT WHEN I came across some of my husband's soccer trophies from when he was a kid. "Throw them away," Jason said. I was horrified. Someday, I wanted to be able to show these to our kids. Jason rolled his eyes. He explained that these were not special trophies, they were "hustle awards." I had never heard the term before. He said the hustle award is what you give a kid who's warmed the bench all season for good sportsmanship. This only made me want to keep the trophies all the more. Only a few of us will ever tap into the magical alchemy of biology, talent, and opportunity. Those people will become ballet dancers and Olympians, doctors and opera singers. The rest of us, if we work hard and are good sports about all the ways in which we fall short, will get the hustle award. In fact, I'm counting on it.

Becoming a working writer has been the most exciting thing that has ever happened to me. My assignments as a journalist for such magazines as *Newsweek* and the *New York Times Magazine* have introduced me to some of the most interesting people I could hope to meet. I've had the opportunity to travel to more of the world than I ever thought possible. I've interviewed priests, politicians, doctors, movie stars, musicians, and the occasional athlete. I've written a novel, three nonfiction books, and five children's books. And not once, in all my years of schooling, from kindergarten to college, did any teacher or professor ever tell me that I should be a writer.

I started reading at four. I remember being tested in the New York City public school system and being thrilled that in first grade, I was reading at a fifth-grade level and in second grade, at a seventh-grade level. My parents were Panamanian immigrants who worked hard to avoid serving up the dish we feared more than any other, "air pudding and nothing pie." But my mother got me a library card as soon as I was old enough to have one. Around the time I was seven, the Reading Is Fundamental program was started, and I began to read with a vengeance.

I don't remember how many books you were required to read to get a free book, but I do remember reading a book a day until finally the librarian said I was over my limit of free books. But the Reading Is Fundamental program worked. Throughout elementary school, I wrote silly brain-twister poems on the spot. This became a party trick with my extended family. My cousins and aunts and uncles would tell people, "Watch her, she can write a poem about you on the spot." I often brought these poems to school, but my teachers did not seem particularly impressed. Our classrooms were crowded, and like so many writers, I was quiet. I know now that I was seeking encouragement, but I can't say I ever asked for affirmation out loud. Like Lana Turner at a Hollywood malt shop, I was hoping to be discovered in the classroom. But I never was.

In sixth grade, I started a newspaper. In high school, and later in college, I began to write for *New Youth Connections,* a teen newspaper in New York City, which remains one of the best professional experiences I've ever had. In high school, I won a scholarship to a program for aspiring minority journalists. The program consisted of two weeks at a university, taking classes in journalism and reporting actual stories that would be published in a special version of the college paper. I worked hard those two weeks, and I met Michael Trotman, the first person who ever told me I was talented. He was a copy editor at the *Home News* in New Brunswick, New Jersey. Michael had not been the editor I was originally assigned to, but I badgered him until he read my stories.

Michael and I are friends to this day; and in that friendship, I see the seeds of my own confidence. By reaching out to him, I was beginning to discover the art of choosing myself, of realizing that my dream of being a writer was not going to be placed on my head like a hat or a crown: "You are now a writer!" But rather, it is something you must decide for yourself, then present it to the world: "I am a writer!" As scary as that may be.

Despite the encouragement I received from Michael, and my own bubbling writerly hopes, I did not yet see myself as an aspiring journalist. I saw myself as an aspirant to the middle class. I had been poor all my life, and I had only one goal: To go to college and not be poor. The two professions that I could imagine for myself were doctor and lawyer. Lacking the desire to be a doctor, I set myself on a pre-law track.

Then I went to Simon's Rock College, a college for kids who want to begin their education early. I was sixteen and had just completed the eleventh grade. While other kids complained about the food, I remember thinking how much food there was. Every meal was a feast. I was so grateful after bouncing from parent to parent—with step-parent drama in between—to have three meals a day and a safe place to sleep. I remember sizing up the other students, seeing if there was anybody I couldn't take. Then I came to the embarrassed realization that this was not a place I would have to fight my way out of. But the biggest surprise to me was the writing. It was constant. I wrote five papers a week for every subject from literature to history to Russian and Spanish. And because I was from poor schools and I was determined not to be stuck with the B's and C's I was being handed, I was constantly rewriting papers as well. Roughly, twenty papers a month—some rewritten twice or three times—for four years. At the end of four years, I was a writer. It sounds like a simplification, but really, it's not. I was waiting to be chosen. I was hoping that someone would see in me a literary gift. What my teachers at Simon's Rock gave me was more than the permission I was seeking; they gave me the practice of being a writer.

My requirements at Simon's Rock were the beginning of the life I now lead. A thousand papers, a thousand times back to this place where I write to you now: the computer, the blank screen, the page count—the edict to "say something!"—and the quiet task of figuring out what, where, when, who, and how.

I spend a lot of time visiting schools, and I correspond with a fair number of students through my Web site. I try to be the voice of encouragement that I never had. But I also try to tell students and grown-up aspiring writers alike that validation—encouragement—is only a start. The business of writing and the art of writing are remarkably monotonous in tone. You write and you write and you write.

The minute you first register the thought that you would like to be a writer—not just write the errant poem or occasional short story—but the moment you declare your ambition to yourself is a declaration of faith. In a way, it's not too dissimilar from taking religious orders. "I'd like to be a nun," you might as well say. "Oh really?" someone, maybe the Mother Superior, says. Then the questioning begins. The questioning and the doubts. How strong is your faith? How deep is your talent? All along the way, the Mother Superiors of your teachers, the publishing industry, your own insecurity, your competitive peers, your well-meaning and highly critical peers, your family, your friends, will cast doubt on your ambition. There are a hundred ways to work through these doubts—many of them surprisingly technical. Writing, it turns out, has a lot in common with bricklaying. But there are esoteric questions. Ones that aren't as easily displaced by good, solid lessons on form, dialogue, plot, and scenes. Among them, I think, is the question "Who cares? What do you have to say that will be of interest to anybody?"

As a Panamanian-born, American-raised daughter of immigrants, I return constantly, in my writing, to the notion of biculturality. Not only what it means in my specific case, but how it can be applied, like an allegory, in many different ways. But I have also become increasingly aware that as a first-generation American writer, I've taken many things for granted. Mostly the confidence that comes with being raised in the United States. Ten years ago, I would have never admitted to any confidence in my writing. Even now, as I struggle to finish my latest project, the words *terror, failure,* and *drawn and quartered,* flash across my mind on a daily basis. But I'm published. Perhaps more important, I write. I write almost every day. That's what takes confidence.

What I think is important to remember, especially for those of us with ties to other countries, is that as American writers we begin with tremendous gifts. We live in a country of literacy with literally thousands of outlets for telling our stories; from big publishing houses to small, independent presses, from college literary magazines to underground 'zines and homemade Web pages. But to connect to my first point, we live in a country that has acknowledged, in ways small and large, that every culture has a story to tell.

The Indian-American author Bharati Mukherjee recently wrote:

> I published my first short story when I was a teenager in Calcutta. It concerned Napoleon's final days on St. Helena. That story was followed by Marie Antoinette awaiting the guillotine, then others featuring assorted figures from Roman history. Those first "gleanings" were testimonies to the inflexible standards of British schooling for girls from "elite" families attending an Irish convent school. The Overseas Cambridge curricula transcended borders and continents; we could have been in Hong Kong, Johannesburg, Adelaide, or Port-of-Spain—wherever local standards were considered slack or non-existent—and turned out the same.
>
> The whole point was, Calcutta (or wherever) did not exist. We did not have interesting lives. Our own cultures were vaguely shameful, and certainly not fit subjects for serious literature. . . . I mention these long-ago em-

barrassments only to make the point that I
considered myself a writer from an early age. I
don't doubt that I would have been a writer if
I had married the "suitable boy" selected by
my father and had never left India. The kind of
writer I became, however, has more to do with
coming to America and the Writers Workshop
at the University of Iowa, marrying a fellow
student (an American-born Canadian) and
moving with him to Canada. . . . We returned
to the United States when we were both 40
years of age. ["On Being an American Writer."
Writers on America. International Information
Programs, U.S. Dept. of State].

Even when you convince yourself that you have a
story to tell, that you will write your way into the roaring
Tower of Babel that is American literature, there are critics from without that are as vocal and powerful as the critics from within. I have been a professional writer for more
than ten years now, and I can count on rejection as a dia-
betic counts on an insulin shot. I don't like it. I wouldn't
choose it. But it is part and parcel of the life I'm leading.
At best, your work is criticized by a smart editor who helps
you become a better writer. Yet even when the editor is
smart, it still hurts.

Not too long ago, an article that I'd been counting on, financially and professionally, a feature for a major national magazine, was in its third round of revision. It was three days before Christmas, and the editor called me on my cell phone. "I hate it!" she said. Blinking back the tears and trying not to collapse, wailing, in aisle five of the Rite Aid drugstore, I asked, "Can you tell me what you hate?" She said, "I hate all of it! Fix it!" Ten minutes later, the phone rang again. The editor said, "I forgot to tell you, the second paragraph was truly awful. Really, really boring. I hated it." A week after Christmas, I sat with my budget and made a contingency plan in case the piece could not be salvaged, and I was not going to be paid. Then I sat down and wrote my heart out. Unsure of what to do with "I hated it" and "Really, really boring," I decided to try to rewrite the piece as if I were convincing my coolest friend that the topic of my article was the next hot thing. I also did some historical research to place my subject in context, to help convince my imaginary cool friend that I knew what I was writing about. A week after I handed in the revision, the editor called me. "I love it. It's perfect. Just what I wanted you to do."

Sometimes, in my career, it has seemed that the desire to be a writer—a desire that keeps me up at night and makes me wake up, panting—was the only thing I had going for me. I keep working. My writing is increasingly a more polished variation on the same quiet prose that I wrote long ago. But I take great pleasure in doing it. I go at it every day, although I do not necessarily write every day. Some days I just take notes. Some days, I read books. Some days, I send an e-mail to my husband or a friend about something I am thinking of writing about and I say, "Does this interest you?"

I am not a fancy writer. When my first book, *Mama's Girl,* was published, my brother was in prison and would call me, collect, with fellow inmates who had also read my book. Each and every one of these inmates said to me, "What I like about your book is there are no big words." This is something that I eventually began to take as a compliment. In many ways, I'm still the same writer I was as a student: simple, no fireworks or literary wordplay. I compared myself to flashier students in my creative writing courses, and I used to leave class feeling like a lump of oatmeal. The funny thing is that my own success has taught me there are a lot of people who like oatmeal.

Knocked Off Balance

THE FIRST TIME I TRIED KICKBOXING, I THOUGHT IT was the most miserable sixty minutes I'd ever paid good money for. The jump-rope drills left me panting for air. Float like a butterfly, sting like a bee? I punched like a girl and tripped over my own shoelaces during the most simple combinations. I kept staring at the clock; and when it was over, my gym clothes were so sweaty I could wring water out of them. Ultimately, it was vanity, not bravery, that made me try kickboxing again. I used to spend hours on the elliptical, and the machine told me I burned a gazillion calories a day. But I never sweated as much as I had during kickboxing. I went back because I wanted that sweat, and I could visualize myself literally knocking off the pounds.

Three years later, I think about my kickboxing workouts in a very different way. I go to class, lace up my gloves, throw a few jabs, then hold up sparring pads against my hip so my partner can drop-kick me Jackie Chan style. I still love what it does for my waistline, but what I love even more is what it does for my equilibrium. For so long, yoga was what I did when I wanted to recharge. I still do yoga. I love the poses and the meditation. Twice a week, I *om* my way to a place of tremendous peace. However, I've learned that kickboxing does exactly the same thing in a very different way. It knocks me off balance, literally and figuratively. It forces me to find center with every punch thrown and received. It's an invigorating and powerful reminder that I am strong and that if I dig deep enough I can face any challenge.

It is Wednesday morning at Redwood's Boxing Studio in Venice. My teacher Redwood is thirtyish, ornery, egotistical, militaristic, charming, and strong. He holds the pads while I cross, jab, cross, jab him across the room. In

fifteen minutes, I am begging for mercy. He is wearing
street clothes and doesn't break a sweat. He is a strange hy-
brid. Part Muhammad Ali. Part Colin Powell.

There are three of us working out in the gym. One
guy, dirty blond, muscular, drop lifts a spectactular amount
of weights. Another girl, small, lithe like a dancer, does
one smooth round kick after another. And I am jumping
rope.

"Come summer, I want to do kali," I say noncha-
lantly. "That is, if you can teach me."

"If I can teach you?" He smiles. He loves a challenge
and he loves the insult hidden within. "What do you
know about kali, Grasshopper?"

I pause. What I know about kali, the Filipino art of
stick fighting, is that I saw Ben Affleck do it in the movie
Daredevil.

Do I fess up the truth? Or try to fake the martial art
funk? I tell him about the Ben Affleck movie.

He screams, like Bruce Lee about to jump into the air
and land a kick that will knock me flat. "You come into
my studio talking about kali and Ben Affleck?" He is kiss-
ing distance now and barking orders in my ear. "Stop
watching Ben Affleck movies! Start running forty-five
minutes a day! Stop eating bread! Stop with the pasta, the
rice. Then we can talk about kali."

For a very long time, I did not understand why Redwood was all over my diet like, well, white on rice. Now I realize that he feels the same way about me that the colorist I see twice a year feels about me. Since I walk around half the year with my color half outgrown, my colorist doesn't want me to tell people I'm her client. And since I won't quit carbs and become the lean, mean fighting machine that Redwood wants me to be, I am not a walking advertisement for his skills as a trainer.

I grab two imaginary sticks from the air, "I still want to do kali."

He puts two five-pound weights in my hand and orders me to box the air: 200 crosses, 200 jabs. "Maybe by summer."

I perk up, "Summer?"

He gives me a devilish smile. "What you don't know, Grasshopper, is that within these four walls, summer will never come."

～

It was summer and kali was far from my mind, when my husband and I moved to Los Angeles and I began a job as a junior writer on a television sitcom. The writer's room, I come to learn, is a boxing ring, and you are not so much fighting the other writers as you are fighting yourself: your own fear, your own sense of timing, the constant and relentless pressure to be funny. The strange thing is that I got my job as a sitcom writer in the least go-getter fashion possible. I had just finished book tour and was at home, parked on the couch, chilling out to a week-long marathon session of Mary Tyler Moore on DVD. I remember thinking, "I wonder if I could ever write for a TV show?" Then a couple of days later, the phone rang. It was my manager calling from Los Angeles. She had spoken to a producer who had read my book and wanted to know if I wanted to write for a comedy about four professional women called *Girlfriends.* Almost haughtily, my manager had told the producer no. "Veronica doesn't write for TV, she writes *novels.*"

This of course conjures up images of Virginia Woolf in a country cottage in England. I was on the couch, in Philadelphia, watching Mary Tyler Moore. As it was, my husband's company was based in Los Angeles, and they had made him an offer he couldn't refuse. I was planning to go west with him, unemployed. Call her back, I urged my manager. I had just finished watching one of my favorite episodes, the one where Mary is being audited and the IRS guy falls in love with her. Genius. By all means, I wanted to give TV writing a shot.

The next thing I knew I was on the Paramount lot sitting in a room with eight of the funniest people I have ever met. It didn't hurt that on the stage next door Jim

Carrey and Meryl Streep were filming *A Series of Unfortunate Events* based on the books by Lemony Snicket, which I absolutely loved. But I soon learned that it was one thing to write a novel that made people laugh and cry. It was quite another thing to write a script with three solid jokes per page. I started my new job at *Girlfriends* and proceeded to fall flat on my face.

And not in the funny way.

I had always thought of myself as funny. My girlfriends thought I was a laugh riot. My husband is convinced that I am the second coming of Lucille Ball. These people, "the professionally funny people," were nowhere near as impressed. I pitched joke after joke and I learned something. Not being funny actually has a smell. It's akin to the smell of rotten eggs and I reeked of it. On one particularly horrible day, when I pitched something that was so miserable, my boss rolled her eyes and suggested we all take a lunch break, everyone went out to lunch without me. Lest you think I'm on the sensitive side, after lunch one of my colleagues came up to me and said, "You're probably feeling really bad about that pitch." I assured him I was. He went onto say, "Yeah, that's what we were all saying when we were out at lunch. She probably knows how much it sucked."

As I suffered through my own personal version of *Mean Girls,* I learned a few things. One was that outside of elementary school, nobody likes knock-knock jokes. Mostly, I laughed more than I ever had at any job in my life. I also learned that comedy is a serious business. There was many a night when we all wanted to go home and we couldn't, because we could not send in the script we were shooting that week until we'd written one last joke. To top it off, no ordinary joke would do. It needed to be a joke that would make the whole room burst out laughing. As one of my colleagues once remarked at the end of a very long day, "It's hell when the funny dogs are chasing you."

Then six months into the most ha-ha year of my life, I had a breast cancer scare. I was sitting in the bedroom, blow-drying my hair when I realized that my T-shirt was stuck to my breasts. I pulled it off and it hurt. I was lactacting or something. My breasts had shiny, garish cuts like someone had sliced them with a penknife. In classic comedy writer fashion, I went into the kitchen and cracked a joke. "Look, weeping mammaries," I remarked to my husband. And like a good comedy writer's spouse, he laughed as he drove me to the emergency room. Even though he was terrified.

The problem was that I'd already been playing chicken with a suspicious lump in my left breast. Just a few months before, my OB-GYN had discovered a small, hard mass in my breast. "It's the size of a BB," he had said, guiding my hand over the lump. "When you move to California, if it becomes the size of a chickpea, call a doctor right away." It seemed like a simple directive to follow. But it turned out to be a kind of curse. Every month my husband and I played "find the lump." Every month we asked ourselves if it was a BB or a chickpea. And every month we agreed that we had no idea. We felt like a couple being booted off of *The Newlywed Show* for insufficient breast knowledge. The mysterious "leakage," as we began to call it, only complicated matters.

The stigmata of the breasts only made things worse. We didn't have local doctors and so I called a woman that I'd read about in a magazine where she was pictured, talking about her practice and modeling the fall fashions. She turned out to have the bedside manner of a pet tarantula. After two mammograms and an ultrasound, and my breasts spontaneously leaking for weeks on end, I confessed that I was scared. My grandmother had died of breast cancer. The doctor looked at me, her face a mask of boredom and indifference. "I have no idea what's wrong with you," she said. "For all I know, you could have cancer in one breast and some strange freak infection in the other." Some strange freak infection? I never saw her again.

It was about this time, when I no longer felt like going to work and being funny that I realized I had to make a decision. Either I was going to give in to the misery I was feeling or I was going to work as hard at being healthy as I had worked at being funny. I chose the latter. I busted my butt and found a great doctor. And it was under this doctor's care, that I made the decision to have a lumpectomy. It was a painful surgery and a painful recovery, but it helped me to realize that while I did have a "strange freak infection," I did not have cancer.

"All the world's a stage," Shakespeare said. We are all starring in our own sitcoms is what I want to tell you. Mary Tyler Moore had hers. I have mine. You have yours. What I want you to know is that when things are good, when things are not good, when things really suck, remember this: You are writing the script, but you don't have to write it alone. There is no Wizard of Funny, raining down jokes like bucketfuls of gold on the soundstages across Tinsel Town. There is only this: nine, maybe ten comedy writers in a windowless room on the back lot of a studio, trying to make each other laugh. Pick the comedy writers for your show. Find the ten people you can count on to infuse every episode of your life with humor and drama and wackiness and pathos. Don't turn away from them if they fail on the first or forty-first try. Remember that on a professional sitcom, it can take hours to write one really good joke. I know who the comedy writers are in my life. And I know that when I was sick, when I was afraid, they were the people who kept me on the air.

I could not box during the months after my surgery. And I missed it. Kickboxing makes me feel strong. And it's such good therapy. I've never forgotten the episode of *The Jeffersons* in which Louise and George go to couples therapy and ending up batting each other with foam paddles. Hitting someone and being hit is a huge deal for most of us who suffer from a chronic case of nice-girl disease. In all the kickboxing classes I've taken, the emphasis is on form, not impact—you're not supposed to hit someone so hard that it hurts. But the fact is, when someone throws ten punches, even soft ones, to your stomach—it's startling, if not exactly painful. When I'm holding an arm guard and someone throws a roundhouse kick so powerful that the guard goes flying out of my hand, I still quiver, ever so slightly, in my sneakers.

The thing that studying kickboxing has taught me, though, is that this is life. You're going to get hit—emotionally and mentally. Not a week in my life goes by when something doesn't startle me as much as a few punches to the gut: be it a disappointing work rejection or a disagreement with a family member or something as seemingly innocuous as my car needing to go to the repair shop. Certainly, there are times when a broken car and all the inherent expense is enough to make me feel like someone's knocked the wind out of me. Kickboxing reminds me that I can take it.

The flip side to learning how to take a punch is, of course, learning how to throw one. If it's true that sometimes when I'm sparring with a partner, it's all I can do not to whimper, "Ow, Ow, Ow." It's helped my feelings of fear to remember that I don't come to class solely to be a human punching bag. I steel myself through sparring sessions with the knowledge that, in just a few minutes, I will be hitting the other person back. This, I assure you, is no big threat. Anyone who has boxed with me will tell you that I still punch like a girl. I don't care. It's incredibly symbolic for me to lift my arms and throw a punch. Sometimes I look at my hands after I've landed a particularly nice jab or cross and I think this is what it must have felt like when Peter Parker realized that his fingers could shoot spiderwebs.

I used to think that being a nice girl was something to be proud of. Growing up, I was always told to be good. And even more, to be careful of making enemies. The problem was that very early on, I began to confuse nice girl with doormat. When I was in the eighth grade, my best friend stole my boyfriend. Four years later as a freshman in college, new boyfriend, new best friend, it happened again. What's the old saying? Fool me once, shame on you. Fool me twice, shame on me. It would take me nearly ten years to figure that out.

By my mid-twenties, I was on a fast track to martyr-dom. One weekend, I let a friend borrow an application for an important writing award. She said she'd photocopy it and leave it in my mailbox that afternoon. Then she conveniently forgot to return it—and didn't return my frantic calls—until Wednesday, a full forty-eight hours af-ter the application was past due. She had a million excuses and apologies, but when she became a finalist for the award, her smile was as wicked as any character out of the Brothers Grimm. Sometimes I thought I was crazy, the way it seemed that the people who were meanest to me were the people who called themselves my best friends.

Finally, I reached a breaking point. Gina had been my pal since high school. We were so proud of how far we'd come, girls from the barrio—she was an investment banker and I was a writer for a national news magazine. I thought we'd be friends until we were old ladies in rock-ing chairs. A full-tilt glamour puss, Gina had always loved having me around when I was the mousy girl in baggy clothes. But when I started dressing better and finally learned how to apply a little makeup, not only was she surprised at the attention I got when we went out but she took huge swipes at my self-esteem. "It's so hilarious to me that these guys think you've got it going on," she said, one night. "I remember when you had no money and wore my hand-me-downs. Everyone here thinks you're something special but I know who you really are, the poor girl who never had anything."

I don't know what it was about the comment that served as such a wake up call. I had heard similarly harsh comments from women who called themselves my friend before. Maybe it was the spirit of my grandmothers giving me a much needed kick in the rear. But I looked at Gina and although I did not say it, what I thought was, "You are not my friend. You are my enemy." I walked out of the club and never spoke to her again. All of our friends tried to intervene. They said that I was bugging out, that I should give her a chance to explain herself. But I felt like I didn't need to hear her explanations to know that Gina didn't have my best interests at heart. She was happy for me to do well, as long as I didn't threaten her position in the friendship as the most beautiful and the most successful. "Believe what people do, not what they say," my mother has always told me. Now for the first time, I was following her advice and it felt so good. It was like I'd stopped leaving my heart across the front doorstep and was finally standing up for myself, as a woman who deserved respect.

That was more than five years ago. In the years since, I've added other people to the list of enemies—the competitive colleague I caught rifling through my desk one morning when I arrived to work early is near the top. At times, when certain friends are treating me poorly, they are also on my enemy list. There's a term for this, a friend who is in the doghouse with you is a "frenemy." It's not so much a hit list as it is my own effort to grow a backbone. There are boundaries with me now, a line of respect and goodwill. Those who cross it, cross it at their peril.

My grandmother used to say that "bad mind"—people wishing you ill—is worse than *brujería*. And truly, I don't wish these people ill. In fact, I often pray for them. I pray for negative friendships to dissolve peacefully. I pray for work tensions to smooth out amicably. But I do keep a short list in my mind of the people that I know I can't turn my back on. It's a short list, never more than two or three people at a time. (A long list, I think, would be a bad thing. A person has mad issues if she's got enemies all around town.) And eventually people fall off the list. Gina may have been my first enemy, but five years later, the truth is that I hardly ever think about her. She's simply a girl I used to know. That's the real power of distancing yourself from people. It frees both of you to cut your emotional losses and move on.

For a very long time, I've struggled with what Don Miguel Ruiz talks about in the *Four Agreements*. Not taking things personally is one of my biggest life challenges. In the midst of planning my wedding, it felt as if it were impossible not to take everything personally. It was as if that long white dress had a sign taped to the back that said "Kick me." For weeks before the wedding, I spent hours each day fielding comments about everything from my weight to the time of the reception to the seating arrangements and menu. "Bob and weave, girl. Bob and weave," I started telling myself when the phone calls came fast and furious. I began to picture myself in kickboxing class, how I had learned to use my knees, to keep my guard up, to slither like a snake between punches. All my life, I'd admired a pantheon of superheroes. As a kid, it had been Wonder Woman, her golden lasso, her bad-ass invisible plane. As I got older, I added other women to my superhero hall of fame—athletes like Jackie Joyner-Kersee and WNBA star Theresa Weatherspoon, movie characters like Foxy Brown and La Femme Nikita. Kickboxing changed my life because for the very first time, when I got into a tough space emotionally and I needed to channel a butt-kicking diva, the person that I channeled was me.

We are more than we could ever imagine ourselves to be. It's what we tell our children, our partners, our friends. But how often do we tell it to ourselves; and if we do, how often do we prove it? How often do we challenge ourselves to do something new, to try something that feels almost tear-inducingly hard? I am not athletic by nature. I spent my entire high school career trying to convince my gym teachers that I had a rare, yet-to-be-explained menstrual cycle that caused me to bleed four weeks a month. But now, every week, kickboxing is my one brave thing. There is always something new, something hard: knife guards, squat kicks, Pilates push-ups. My kickboxing class reminds me that I am always capable of more, even if it's just a quarter inch higher in my kicks. And my body registers the information as more than just a mental pep talk, it becomes muscle memory. I can feel it in my arms, my legs, my bones.

Which brings me to my final point. Every week, I go to this class. My hamstrings burn through the warmup and my knees ache during the push-up drills. The sparring always scares me, even when I'm paired up with the lightest featherweight in the room. But I do it. I take my hits, I throw a few, and they haven't had to wheel me out of class yet. On the contrary, I float back to my car—feeling if not exactly like Rocky then like these toys I used to love when I was a kid. They were called Weebles, and their selling point was that "Weebles wobble, but they don't fall down." I like to think I'm like that—not just in my body, but in my heart, where it really counts. I wobble. I wobble all the time. But I don't fall down.

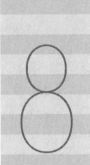

Esther Williams

S HE DOES NOT KNOW ME FROM ADAM, BUT TINK
Bolster, a seventy-four-year-old triathlete, is a god-
dess to me. I was living in Princeton, New Jersey,
when I happened to pick up the free local paper, *The Princeton Packet*. On the front page, there was a picture of an older
woman, looking spry in a bicycle helmet. The caption underneath the picture read, "Even the occasional injury or
broken bone has not stopped Princeton resident Tink Bolster from competing in triathlons." I sat on the front step

of my apartment and I read with awe and wonder about this woman who is living my dream.

Every time I tell someone that I want to do a triathlon, they are impressed. Then I mention that I can't swim and they look at me as if I were a special kind of stupid. But why do people believe that because I can't swim *today* this means that I will *never* be able to swim? My goal is the Kona Half Ironman in Hawaii: a one-plus-mile swim, a thirteen-mile run, and a fifty-six-mile bike ride. I could probably run thirteen miles. I've done two ten-mile races, and I plan on doing a thirteen-mile race this year. But I will have to get up to speed on the bike ride, and I will have to learn how to swim. It had once been my goal to do the Kona Half Ironman for my fortieth birthday. Then along came Tink Bolster, and I realized that forty was such an arbitrary number. Reading about her gave me an extra twenty-four years to get my swimming act together. Twenty-four years. So many of us are on timelines: married by this age, own a house by that age, have kids by this age—or else. My question is, or else what? For me, the key to setting goals is to give myself plenty of time to do it.

I don't know if Tink Bolster would be so impressed by my admiration. "Sometimes, specatators along the way will say things like, 'I hope to be able to do that when I'm half your age,'" she told the *Princeton Packet*. "I know they are trying to be nice, but I'm not Methuselah." What she is, however, is disciplined. I don't know about you, but I look for role models in discipline wherever I can find them. Nothing is more tiresome to me than the actress with washboard abs and sinewy biceps who says she eats whatever she wants and never exercises. What can I do with tales of good genetics and natural-born talent when I am so sorely lacking in either? Perhaps it's slightly puritanical of me, but give me the grit and the dirt of hard work. Tell me exactly what "giving two hundred percent" entails: What do you do? At what time? For how long?

Tink Bolster gets up every day at five A.M. and swims two to three thousand yards. Then she runs at least three miles. By 8:30 in the morning, she's done two of her three training activities. In addition, she rides her bike 180 to 250 miles a week. She mounts her bike on a stationary trainer in the winter and rides outside in the summer. It's an amazing lesson in discipline for someone who's twenty-four or seventy-four. It's also, she told the *Packet,* fun. "I like the training," she says. "I'm not beating myself into the ground. In a race, I'm knocking myself out. It's hard. But when I'm done, I'm thinking, 'Wasn't it good that I did that?' It's good for the mind, soul, and body."

I have a little bit of an idea of how she feels. I learned to run by walking a block and jogging a block. When I started, I couldn't do more than two blocks at a time. Along the way, different friends who visited me—my friend Cassandra, my friend Liba, my friend Paul—joined me in my runs and helped me cover greater distances. I lived in Brooklyn Heights at the time, and my first goal was to run to the promenade that overlooks the East River. My next goal was to run from my house to the end of the promenade. This short run was especially satisfying because I passed the Statue of Liberty each way. "Wave to the lady," I'd tell myself, as I chug-chugged along. My final goal was to run from my house, over the Brooklyn Bridge into Manhattan and back. When I reached that goal, I felt like I could do anything.

Still, running was never easy for me. I ran so slow that my friends joked that what I was doing was "wogging"— more walking than jogging. And although I ran two ten-mile races, I never ran with ease, I ran "hard," flinging myself like a very slow Frisbee toward the finish line. A few months ago when I decided to start running seriously again, I decided to work with a trainer. I'd read about Aimee Carpenter in *Marie Claire* magazine, and I was surprised when I sent her an e-mail that it was Aimee herself who called me back. Aimee explained that her training technique was a mixture of running and hiking, but the most amazing thing was, she did the runs with you.

In the months that I've been training with Aimee, I've felt my running transform. I don't pound the pavement anymore. I've stopped being so macho about not using my inhaler, so my breathing is getting better. Moreover, when I haven't run in a few days, I begin to crave it. Recently, Aimee and I have had to move our running time from seven A.M. to six A.M. This means that I need to be up at five, out of my house by 5:30. The first morning I woke up that early, I thought, "Aw hella. It's been fun, but I'm so over this." I hate leaving the house when it's dark outside, but I turned on my car stero, pumped up my favorite album by the Roots and by the time I met Aimee at six, I was feeling semiawake. For the first few blocks, it was still dark outside, which made me cranky. But by the time we reached my big hill on Maple, the sun was coming out. It felt like I was running into the sunrise. By 6:45, I'd run three-point-two miles and I was feeling like Tink Bolster. It's a good feeling when you know the day has barely started and you've been kicking butt for hours.

In an effort to get closer to my goal of learning how to swim, I've been taking water aerobics classes. This sounds like a simple enough thing, but it took me nearly a year to actually take a class. I was convinced that water aerobics actually involved swimming; and every time I called the gym to ask if I needed to know how to swim in order to take the class, the disaffected slacker who worked the front desk said, "Uh, I don't think so." I could have shown up for a class and asked the teacher. I could have gone to the pool area and seen that the deepest end of the gym pool is only five feet. But I was so intimidated that I never did.

Then, about a year ago, I was visiting Rancho La Puerta, one of my favorite spas in Baja California. I knew the pool there wasn't deep so I showed up for a lunchtime water aerobics class. I was amazed by all the women gathered around the pool. They were all older than me by twenty, thirty, forty years. But they were beautiful. "Do you know those kind of older women who swim every day?" a friend had once asked me. "I want to be like them." I did not know what she meant at the time, but sitting by the pool at the ranch, I knew immediately. It was as if you were getting into the water with every movie star you'd ever seen on Turner Classic Movies. I wanted to say, "Oh my, there goes Myrna Loy at eighty. There's Barbara Stanwyck at seventy-five. Diahann Carroll at seventy." The women were older, but they were not old. Each of them was dressed in sleek maillots and some of them wore bathing caps. Sure, some of them were overweight. Some of them were less fit than others. But as a rule, they were what used to be called a tall, cool drink of water.

In that first water aerobics class, I sometimes struggled to follow the teacher's directions. My behind, bootylicious as it might be, is like an anchor. I could probably dock the *QE2* at port. The women in my class were so warm, so helpful. They whispered encouragement and threw me extra noodles and flashed me big smiles and the thumbs-up sign whenever I got the hang of a particularly tricky move. At the end of the class, the teacher said, "Now, we'll do Esther Williams." I had no idea what she was talking about. But somebody pulled me into a circle as the group split into two. We counted off every other person; one, two; one, two. Then the ones ran really quickly and held on tight as the twos threw their legs in the air like Radio City Hall rockettes. Then the twos ran very quickly and the ones got to do a water dance routine. And when the music stopped, we all collapsed into a fit of laughter that carried us out of the pool, into the changing room and into the rest of the day.

I did not know much about Esther Williams before I started taking water aerobics. I knew that she had made several movies in the pool of the Raleigh Hotel, my favorite place to stay in Miami. What I have learned about Esther Williams since is that she did not pursue a film career because when she was young, she couldn't act, she couldn't dance, and she couldn't sing. What happened is that Hollywood came looking for a girl, an athlete, to make into a movie star. She was the high school swimming champion of Los Angeles who had qualified for a berth on the Olympic swim team but was cheated out of her shot at the gold when the United States boycotted the games in 1940. In that same year, she pioneered a sport—synchronized swimming—and made the sport famous in movies like *Dangerous When Wet.* What she lacked in acting ability, she made up for in hard work and became one of the biggest box-office draws of her day. She survived sexual abuse as a teen and two failed marriages with an absolutely stunning amount of aplomb. She was not intimidated by her co-stars. Gene Kelly, her paramour in *Take Me out to the Ballgame* was no Esther Williams fan. "As much as Kelly resented the fact that I was not a dancer, he resented my height even more," she said. And when Kelly gave her the business, she cut through all the subterfuge with her unusually blunt take on things. "Gene," she said. "I have perfect proportions in a swimsuit and that's why I'm making movies at MGM. I'm sorry that my physique doesn't fit in with your plans." When an affair with another co-star, Jeff Chandler, disintegrated at the realization that he was a cross-dresser, Williams let him know that "I can't be married to a matron." And commenting on her lover's outfit, she added, "Jeff, you're too big for polka dots."

I play Esther Williams, in my water aerobics class, every chance I get. Lately, I've been making my way down to the deep end of the pool. I still need two noodles to float, but I am falling in love with the weightlessness that I feel in the water. It's as if there were nothing to do and nowhere to be. When I am leaning back and the water is carrying me, it is the closest I have ever felt to God's grace.

It is probably no accident that increasingly my definition of grace is tied to the image of water. I let the water carry me, and I am reminded that I am not in this world alone. I drive to the ocean because it is a portrait in perspective, a powerful reminder of all the little things that do not matter. So while I learn to be comfortable in the water, while I work my way up to swimming, I am also working on that most particular of grace notes: forgiveness. Whenever I got angry, I had a friend who used to say "Now I see the Panamanian in you." To tell the truth, I think he thought it was sexy when I went off the handle, nostrils flaring and eyes ablaze. Isn't that part of the Latina archetype—the way we can boil like a pot of Cuban coffee, our hearts brewing a rage that is dark, strong, and bitter? And while it is true that it is in our spirit to make love as easily as we make war, what happens to the anger that we cannot let go? The dregs of coffee that remain burned to the pot?

We know that unresolved anger isn't good for the soul. It can cause us to become distrustful of others, shutting them out when we should be letting them in. But wounds that don't heal also have physical effects. In a groundbreaking study, dubbed "The Forgiveness Project," doctors at Stanford University found that long-held grudges and resentment can have serious long-term effects on our health: high blood pressure as well as stresses on the cardiovascular and immune systems.

Ultimately, offering up forgiveness is only half of the equation. If you want to heal a relationship, the other person has to be willing to meet you halfway. You can forgive, but not accept, an abusive partner back into your life if he doesn't get counseling. You can forgive, but not accept, the girlfriend who is always borrowing money if she doesn't take serious steps to rectify her financial situation. Forgiveness is a gift that must be offered without strings or expectations. It's not a magic wand that will fix other people. But it will—and can—lighten your load. Freeing up the time and energy you spend on anger, hurt, resentment, and blame so that you can move on with your life.

Maybe you think this doesn't relate to you. You're not like your *tia* Rosa who has not spoken to her sister in twenty years but refuses to pick up the phone. You're not like your friend Claudia who lost the love of her life to her so-called best friend. You don't have major issues with people. Then think about this: Maybe the person you need to forgive is yourself.

For a long time, I didn't notice how often I would

beat myself up. Until one day on the phone, a friend said, "Wow. You are hard on yourself." Suddenly, I saw that self-criticism had become such a regular part of my life that I didn't notice the constant stream of "you screwed ups" in my head.

I look at my girlfriends and I know I'm not alone. One of my friends is furious at herself for not losing those last fifteen pounds. Another woman I know is angry at herself for not starting the screenplay she always dreamed about writing. I have a friend who has yet to forgive herself for dating a guy who used to beat her up, even though she dated him years ago.

Here's a suggestion. Tonight, before you go to bed, instead of criticizing yourself, look in the mirror and congratulate yourself. Forgive yourself for something, then look just as hard to find something worth praising. Maybe you haven't lost the weight you want to, but you are a terrific mother and wife. Maybe you speak Spanish like a *gringa,* but you have tremendous pride in your *patria.* Then, the next night, write down a list of five people who have hurt you and then, one by one, release them. Burn the list, or rip it up and throw it away. You may have been hurt. You may have been wronged in the most egregious ways. But there is a powerful strength in forgiveness. It is a feather, a silk parachute, the very wings on which we fly from our past into our present and toward our future.

Grace has always been one of my favorite words. I had an aunt named Grace, whom I loved. She never seemed to follow any time schedule. She might arrive in July with an armful of Christmas presents. She might show up on an ordinary spring day with a birthday surprise, although my brother's birthday is in July and mine is in October. She never showed up empty-handed, and in the landscape of a childhood where money was always tight, an aunt who was so giving was a miraculous thing.

Grace, Anne Lamott says, meets you where you are but does not leave you where she found you. I could say the same thing about the college that I attended. My education was an exercise in grace: of scholarships and of a student loan officer who always found the money for me to stay in school, of professors who made personal loans for my education and of staff members who invited me into their homes when I could not afford to return to my own. It's because of this that I concentrate the bulk of my financial giving to my college.

Four years ago, I became a philanthropist. A fact that shocks me even now, as I neither come from money nor make a ton of it today. Yet over a three-year giving campaign, with the help of my former employer's matching gifts program, I was able to endow a study room, in my grandmother's name, in the college library of my alma mater, Simon's Rock in Great Barrington, Massachusetts.

For roughly the cost of a Prada dress, handbag, and shoes, I was able to create a legacy that lasts and lasts. My favorite teacher goes to my grandmother's room to read in her spare time. I visit the campus, and there are students in there studying, daydreaming, and whispering head to head.

As a student at a small school, I was surrounded by the names of the college's "friends"—on the scholarships I received and on the buildings in which I lived and attended class. When I made a gift of $5,000 (paid over three years, at about $140 a month and matched by my company), I added my name and my grandmother's to the mix. The plaque reads "Gift of Veronica Chambers '87. In loving memory of Flora Jean Baptiste."

I know that a lot of people couldn't care less about giving money to their college. We all get those obnoxious alumni bulletins with the Christmas-letter reports about who has just gotten married, been short-listed for the Nobel prize in physics, made their first million. What does a hundred dollars really mean to your old college anyway? I thought pretty much the same thing—I mean, I just paid off my student loans last year. For a long time, I thought my own sad bank balance was a more worthy charitable fund than the college's annual fund-raising drive.

Then I had dinner with Bernard Rodgers, then the dean of my college. Because I was such a nerd in school, I still regularly talk to members of the college faculty. For me, though, my involvement with Simon's Rock is more meaningful than the fact that I've always been a teacher's pet. After growing up in an abusive household, I had gone to college early because it had gotten to the point that I had no place to go—it was either find a school where I could live (boarding school or college) or drop out of high school, find an apartment, and get a job.

Moreover, while Simon's Rock gave me a healthy scholarship, I could not declare myself legally independent. My father's income was counted on for a contribution, but he never ever paid a single dime. Every semester, I sat in the financial aid office, quivering. Every semester, someone at the college figured out a way for me to stay, extra loans were co-signed on my behalf, private gifts were solicited. I loved my education: classes that were never bigger than eight students; plenty of room to design independent studies. An independent study course that I helped design on the Harlem Renaissance is still taught to this day. A truly hippie school, Simon's Rock is the sort of place where a two-hundred-pound girl starred in the dance concert and a four foot, eleven scrappy boy played forward on the basketball team. Sure, sometimes it felt

like Misfit U, but it was a fun, totally nonjudgmental place
to go to school. However, what sealed my loyalty was
the financial commitment the college made to me—
not based on my brilliance. I'd attended seven inner-city
schools by the eleventh grade, and Simon's Rock helped
me because I really wanted to be there and I had no place
else to go.

It always seemed natural to me that once I started
making a good living I would give back to the college. I
had once confided to Bernie, our dean, that someday I
hoped to endow a scholarship in the name of my grandmother. She loved to read. A Martinique woman who
came to Panama to work in the government laundry after the opening of the Canal, she taught herself Spanish
on the job, then taught herself to read English through
the diligent study of comic books and picture westerns.
Bernie explained that the renovation of the library offered
a chance to honor my grandmother in some small way.
For $500 I could have a plaque on a chair. For $1,000, I
could stamp her name on a table. For $5,000, I could get a
study room. All of a sudden, he had made the idea of phi-
lanthropy both personal and tangible. I'm a girl who grew
up in the age of labels—from Jordache jeans in junior
high, to the quest for Gucci, Donna Karan, and Michael
Kors in my twenties. I wanted to put my grandmother's

name on something—and greedily, I wanted more than a chair. I went home, took out my calculator, and began to do the math.

Like everyone else in our country, I am always flooded with requests for money. Each cause seemed worthier than the next—the pediatric AIDS fund, Greenpeace, the neighborhood heating fund, my local food bank. Each month, I would gather all the charity requests and pick one to write a check—maybe I would send $15 or $20. Occasionally, especially around the holidays, I splurged and sent $50. But it was hard to see where that money was really going. The next month, my mailbox would be filled with the same amount of requests, the same anonymous pleas to reach into my pocket and make a difference. By committing to a monthly gift, and having it matched, I would be focusing all my goodwill on one cause. That seemed to make sense. Still, $140 a month was a lot of goodwill for me at the time, and I made the commitment knowing that it would be hard. Some months I was late, some months I cringed as I wrote the check and passed on a weekend away with friends. But I kept thinking about how much my grandmother had inspired me and how she had died before I was old enough to tell her so. I could see that plaque in my head, and it was the proverbial carrot on the stick that kept me going.

I think my dean knew that since I was a struggling young writer, my small gift represented a major commitment to the college. Even before I wrote that first check, I had tried to give back to the school that had given me so much—by teaching writing seminars, sitting on panels during career day, meeting with students. Bernie asked me to serve on the college's board, and that invitation, coupled with my gift, has taught me more than I ever could imagine about the power and influence that even a little money can buy.

As a Simon's Rock board member, I sit four times a year at a long mahogany table in a centuries-old stone house. My colleagues are mostly men, mostly white—some of them are forty years my senior. Sometimes I look around the solid-oak boardroom where we meet and think this looks like a scene out of a sitcom: a dozen well-dressed older, white men; a couple of fashionably dressed corporate white women; and me, a black girl with dreadlocks, dressed in a BCBG sweater dress (I gave up on wearing suits years ago) and duly applying my Nars lipgloss during the breaks. I don't look the part of a college trustee, and most of the time, I certainly don't feel the part. Mostly I feel like Goldie Hawn in *Private Benjamin,* fresh out of beauty college and being ordered to do military maneuvers. But my commitment allows me to make decisions

about curriculum and policy. I join in during heated con-
versations about the future of the college, about how and
where to plant trees that will outlive us all. I help plan
the construction of multimillion-dollar buildings. I've
learned how to read an architect's blueprints and to ask
questions about backup generators and drainage.

At first, I was so intimidated that I hardly said a word.
But as time went on, I grew confident that even though I
am young and not wealthy, unlike many of the members,
who are either parents of alumni, prestigious educators in
their field, administrators, or philanthropists, I went to
the school. I'm the most recent graduate on the board. I
know what the school is like on a day-to-day basis. When
someone argues against the necessity of spending money
on minority recruitment, I speak up. As a black woman, I
know that at a school of three hundred kids, 8 percent
ethnic minorities may sound good on paper, but it actually translates to twenty-four kids—ten black, eight Asian,
and four of other colors. It's a situation that can be tremendously isolating for students of color and guarantees
that every day there are classes taught in which there are
no students of color at all.

I've also gained a tremendous role model. Emily
Fisher, the head of our board, is a petite powerhouse of a
woman who can quiet a room with a single glance. Emily

attended Vassar and Harvard, but she chose to head the board at Simon's Rock because she believes that she can have the most influence at such a young school (it was founded in 1968). I know that Emily is wealthy—the newly built Fisher Science Center was endowed by her—but for the most part, she shows her generosity in ways that people will never see. She doesn't like for there to be dollar figures attached to her name. At the same time, I've seen Emily use her money to make a point. When she believes in something, she funds it, often attaching a challenge grant that promises further funding if the rest of the board joins in the giving.

Watching Emily, I've developed dreams that I never knew could exist. As I get older, I want to expand my philanthropic efforts, and eventually I want to do what she does. I want to head the board of a college or major arts institution. I'm not like the rich young women you read about in *Town & Country,* who chair fashion balls and raise millions of dollars. Being on a board has taught me that the realm of doing good is not relegated to those who are filthy rich or those who choose social services or education as a profession. It thrills me to no end that I learned to stop writing $25 checks and funnel my charitable giving to one organization at a time.

Two years ago, when I got married, my husband and I were asked by several relatives whether we wanted cash as a wedding present. Jason and I decided to ask that any cash gifts be given to the college to fund a scholarship for the Young Writers Summer Program at Simon's Rock. We named it the Dorothy West Scholarship for Young Writers, in honor of the youngest member of the Harlem Renaissance. The scholarship enables one high school student a year to spend the summer in the Berkshires, studying writing and enjoying summer in the country, doing all the things neither of us could afford to do when we were students, like going to hear the Boston Symphony perform at Tanglewood. We've already been able to raise enough money to allow the first student to attend.

Last year, we established a second scholarship, in honor of my paternal grandmother. It's called the Connie Chambers scholarship, and it is awarded to a student majoring in creative writing. It feels like a funny twist of the old union adage, "Vote early, vote often." We've started our philanthropic giving early, we hope to give often, and it definitely feels good.

If one definition of *grace* is giving and another is allowing yourself to be carried, then perhaps a third definition involves simply stepping into the frame. Every year when I lived in New York, I went ice-skating at Rockefeller Center under the twinkling lights of that gi-normous tree. Although I grew up in New York, my Brooklyn neighborhood was a world away from all the glamour of that Manhattan landmark. I watched the ice-skating rink—like so many things that were close, yet so far away—on television in old black-and-white movies in which all the girls were dames and all the fellas were swell. It took me years to make it to Rockefeller Center. Another ten to muster up the courage to join the ice-skaters I watched so admiringly.

I'm a terrible ice-skater and I have to grip the rail the entire hour that I'm on the ice. On my annual outing, I watched the old folks, the young couples, the flocks of children, and the tourists gaze up at the tree. I see the pros in the center of the ice, twirling and jumping through the air. I sing along with the carols piped in over the loudspeaker, and it doesn't matter that I am crawling around the edge of the ice, not much better than the athlete who spends the season warming the bench. I could take lessons. I could go more than once a year. But that would ruin the magic of it all. The one day a year that I go skating is like Christmas: a hurricane of emotion and expectation and hope. Every kid remembers being told that if Christmas came more than once a year it wouldn't be so special. My ice-skating has made me a believer. Dressed in a hot pink wool cloche hat and a matching muffler, I am stylish but uncoordinated. I am, always, a little afraid. But all that matters is that on the ice, as in my own life, I am the star. And the camera that is my mind, my heart, my imagination, has eyes only for me. The irony is that my annual ice-skating expedition and my weekly water aerobics homage to Esther Williams have more than a little in common. In the late 1930s, Sonja Henie starred in a series of successful ice-skating musicals for Twentieth Century Fox. "Melt the ice, get a swimmer, and make it pretty!" was Louis B. Mayer's response. That swimmer was Esther Williams.

PART III

Two for the Road

Traveling Alone

M Y FRIEND ANGELA HAS AN AMAZING CAPACITY FOR rallying people to travel together. Last year, she managed to summon dozens of friends to a thirtieth birthday/millennium bash she threw for herself in Paris. This year, she's planning Christmas in Australia. On the other hand, I have found it nearly impossible to coordinate trips with my friends. Either our schedules don't coordinate or our travel budgets don't mesh; and most of the time, I end up traveling alone. For a long time, this made me feel slightly deficient—not in the midst of the trip; once I'm on a plane or bike or buckled into an automobile, I feel an unparalleled swell of excitement. The hardest part of traveling alone, I've found, isn't feeling lonely in a hotel room or in a restaurant in a foreign city. It's that moment when someone asks you where you're going. You answer. Then the next question is "Who are you going with?" Whenever I answer, "No one, by myself," I always sense an awkwardness that I think is only partially answered. "Oh," they say. A very loaded 'Oh,' that is. It's as if you had just told them you have no boyfriend, you have no friends, you've only recently gotten your wart problem under control, and you live with six cats.

The first major trip I took alone was when I was in my early twenties. I received an unexpected windfall from the first book I wrote, which I dutifully split into impractical, but wholly satisfying, thirds. I spent a third on a used car. With the next small stack of bills, I bought my first painting. I used the remaining funds to finance a two-week photography course in Morocco. I had read about courses through the Santa Fe Photography Workshop, but I'd never been able to afford one. Now that I had the money, I sent them a check right away. I did not consult a friend. I did not ask anyone whether or not it was a good idea. I didn't ask anyone to come along. The course was expensive and as I suspected neither my boyfriend at the time nor my pals had the money or interest in going. But I had studied photography as an undergraduate. While framing the portraits in my senior show, I dreamed of becoming another Margaret Bourke-White, traveling the world and taking pictures for *Life*.

The trip, which was taught by an established woman travel photographer, gave me the chance to play out the fantasy of another life. I shot a good forty rolls of film during those two weeks. I bowed outside of mosques, sipped mint tea with nomad tribes, rode a camel through Casablanca. Sometimes the sunsets were so beautiful, my heart would ache with loneliness. The sheltering sky that Paul Bowles so vividly captured in his novel of the same name was incredibly romantic and while I dreamed of making love in the desert, my deepest desire was simply to share the view with someone. To tug at a lover's sleeve and murmur, "Look at that. Just look at that." But for the most part, I wasn't lonely in Morocco.

When I look back at pictures of myself on that trip—snapped by other students—there is a remarkable peacefulness on my face. Each smile is broad and genuine. The laughs on that trip, even if they were at jokes I told in my head, were all belly deep. Each day—through the bazaars and souks and hand-tiled palaces—was a delight to the senses. There was always something new to see, to smell, to taste. And if I was there alone, what did it matter? I was there, in the thick of life. It wasn't passing me by.

I learned something valuable that trip about traveling alone: It helps to have a prop. My camera was a good friend to me throughout Morocco. As a somewhat shy person, I reach for a book as my first line of defense. But if I'd traveled through Fez, Marakkesh, and Rabat with my head buried in a book, I would've missed so much. The camera forced me to see Morocco, to focus in on the details, to pause before each sight before I scurried away. It was also a mask that hid my face, my shyness, my astonishment, even sometimes, my tears. On another solo vacation, I signed up for a biking tour of Block Island. I'm not much of a cyclist, I learned, as I trailed behind the group and huffed and puffed up the hills. But the bicycle served a similar purpose, forcing me to venture out and see the island, not just loll around on the beach.

I continued to travel, sometimes alone and sometimes with friends, through Europe, South Africa, and, more recently, Asia. I began to believe that there was nothing a travel adventure couldn't cure. The job from Hell, a broken heart, nightmare holidays, the blahs, the blues, and Holly Golightly's "mean reds"—these are like the blues, but ten times worse—could all be fixed by a weekend at a bed and breakfast in the Berkshires or a bowl of noodles slurped in a crowded café in Shanghai. Then I got sick, for real, and I put the travel cure to the test. And the trip that I took, quietly and magnificently, changed my life.

One day I was fine. The next day, I was having hernia surgery. Two months later, I was still sick with complications that baffled even the best doctors. The hernia surgeon sent me to a gynecologist who sent me to a bone specialist who sent me back to the hernia surgeon. Just when I was on the verge of recovery, I got a nasty strain of mono. My tonsils swelled, my ears ached, my throat was so raw I couldn't drink or swallow. Because I have asthma and my throat was so messed up, I developed problems breathing and had to make periodic visits to the hospital to be ventilated. That's when I wasn't visiting the hospitals to be fed through an IV since I couldn't swallow food. Yes, I was a pitiful mess.

As I was working freelance, there was no income. In four months, I'd gone through my savings account. I'd also worn out the welcome of even my closest friends. My doctors prescribed painkillers, bottle after bottle of Vicodin, which I would've sold on the street for grocery money if I had known the value of them. They did precious little to obliterate my pain. I listened to pain management tapes to get up in the morning. By three P.M., I was exhausted and out for the count again. I begged my doctors to give me a timetable. "I haven't worked in ages," I pleaded. "What am I going to do?" My doctor just shook his head. "Rest," he said. "You are very, very sick." So I rested and I cried and I wondered what exactly I had done to deserve this.

By the time I got better, I'd been ill for almost six months. It was spring, which seemed like a good sign. My friend Shandana, who lives in New York, called and invited me to spend a week with her in the Andalucia region in southern Spain. That week, I received two freelance checks that I thought would never come. It was enough to cover two months rent and a plane ticket. Everything else, I decided, could go on my credit card.

I quickly decided that I needed more than a week's vacation. Tooling around online travel sites, I booked three additional weeks of solo travel—to Barcelona, Madrid, and Paris. The week in Andalucia with Shandana was lovely, partly because I knew it was only the beginning of my journey. I saw Shandana and her friend Greg off at the airport, then continued on to Barcelona. There, I adopted Gaudí and Picasso as my travel buddies, visiting all of Gaudí's tripped-out architecture and Picasso's early paintings. Sitting at an outdoor café one afternoon, I ran into my friend Joanne, from New York. We became dinner companions for the remainder of the week—meeting each evening to compare notes, drink wine, and stroll along Las Ramblas. Running into Joanne kept loneliness at bay, refilling my emotional well for the next leg of my trip.

In Madrid, I dove into the world of Diego Velásquez—enraptured by a personal encounter with my favorite painting in the whole world, *Las Meninas.* I ate breakfast and lunch alone in Madrid, though I still found solo restaurant dinners an intimidating project. I would eat dinner early, at five o'clock, or in my hotel room. By the time I got to Paris, I needed no project, no art or architecture to structure my days. I had miraculously reconnected to my oldest friend—myself. I was no longer furious with my body for falling apart on me.

During my illness, I had listened dutifully to audiotapes by Caroline Myss. She talked about how hard it was to keep promises to ourselves. We say we'll drink more water, but we don't. We say we'll get up and go running, but we don't. We'll bend over backward to keep our word to a lover, a friend, an employer, a total stranger even. But a promise to our own self is the hardest to keep. This is why we shouldn't get so frustrated with our bodies when we are ill. We tell ourselves to get better, that we will appreciate our body and treat it well, but our body knows better than to believe us. Our bodies have been silent witnesses as we've broken promise after promise to ourselves. As far as I ever learned, my illness had no simple cause or effect. It wasn't because of smoking or poor diet or anything I had been warned about. But I did know that before my illness, I never took myself seriously as someone who needed care and attention. I promised myself a million things—to try a yoga class, to stop filling my weekends with a gazillion errands, to get up early and watch the sun rise. And I very rarely kept them. Yet, I could be counted on to show up for anyone and everyone who asked.

By the time I got to Paris, I made a decision that I was going to be better to myself. It wasn't going to take another frightening, extended illness for me to take a break or say no or to remember what mattered to me most. It's a promise I've kept and now more than ever, I see travel not only as a step away from the world I live in but a restorative effort, a way to refill my own emotional well.

Six months after Paris, I was negotiating the subways of Shanghai alone, while my friend who lived there was at work. I visited a different wing of the Shanghai Museum each day, spending hours in the café, writing in my journal and sipping tea. I was followed wherever I went—there were not that many black women with dreadlocks in Shanghai—and more than once, I found myself surrounded by groups of men and teenagers, asking me questions and making comments in a language I couldn't understand. But it was part of the journey, and I braved it alone. A year later, I spent a weekend alone in Brussels— eating dinner each night in an elegant café on an old town square, searching out the most exquisite chocolate shop, even flying solo at an outdoor rock concert with thirty thousand screaming fans. Two years later, I traveled through Japan by bullet train. A mostly uneventful ride, though the countryside was gorgeous. Then the train stopped at Nagoya, and I was seated next to a businessman who wanted to practice his English. He was giving a speech at a conference in Hong Kong and asked if he could read it to me. I agreed. It was horrifyingly, stultifyingly boring. But there was something wonderful about being read to, something very Anna and the King of Siam about the way he was at once arrogant and self-assured but desperate for my approval. After he was finished reading, he asked if he could buy me an ice cream cone. I agreed. And for the rest of the ride, we ate our ice cream cones in near silence, like playground friends who needed no words.

There are two wonderful lines from the poem "The Tourist and the Town" by Adrienne Rich:

> *There is a mystery that floats between*
> *The tourist and the town. . . .*

I think of these words often, when I am traveling alone. I hate to be marked as a tourist; I won't open a map on a public street unless my life depends on it. And yet, there is a mark of a tourist that I cannot escape: the carefree expression of one whose tragedies and triumphs are miles, and sometimes continents, away.

A Tribe Called Us

S IT HARD TO TELL WHEN YOU'VE REACHED THE BREAK-
ing point? I know that I'm more beast than woman,
when my husband says those six magic words, "Go get a
massage. I'll pay." Back when I was a single girl and living
alone, I had to learn how to tell when my own inner com-
pass was out of kilter. It usually started when the line between exhaustion and exhilaration began to blur for me.
For months I'd find myself walking the tightrope between
these two emotions. Work was great—I had a writing job

I loved—but the stress was enormous. And after renting the movie *How Stella Got Her Groove Back* three times, I was fairly sure of two things: my obsession with Taye Diggs's behind was becoming a problem, and I was desperate for a retreat with my girlfriends.

Getting face time with my friends is never easy. We cancel lunch with one another, apologize and reschedule so often that it has become an elaborate dance. When I call my friends, it's usually because I need free therapy or I want to gossip about men and clothes. Our days leave little room for anything deeper. For years, I've held a yearly New Year's brunch: Sometimes it would be organized around a clothing swap, sometimes an ad hoc, one-off book club. It took me a while, though, to amp up from a girls' brunch to a proper organized trip.

It was five years ago when I planned my first girls' getaway weekend and the first challenge was figuring out where to go. It needed to be within driving distance (so we could save money by carpooling) and set no one back precious vacation days. A friend suggested a beautiful country farmhouse called Seekonk Pines Inn. It's in the Berkshire Hills, about three hours north and a world away from my New York City frenzy. I went to college in those hills. Since it was off-season and not too chichi, I knew that staying there wouldn't leave any of my three girlfriends with an overdrawn bank account. We decided to rent the entire inn—it's very small—so we could have the place to ourselves.

My friend Sarah, an artist between jobs who was engaged, said yes right away to my invite. But my other two friends, Karen and Linda, were single moms, and I worried that they'd balk. It was hard enough for them to arrange baby-sitting for a night at the movies, much less for a weekend. But it turned out that Karen, a law-office coordinator, and Linda, the mother of nine-year-old twins who runs her own television-production company, needed the trip more than I did. We decided to leave Saturday morning and return Sunday night, one night and two days to reconnect with one another and with ourselves.

Karen and I drove up to the inn, Linda and Sarah met us there; our schedules were too hectic for a carpool. I'd brought the two girl-getaway musts: champagne and chocolate. I even made dinner reservations at a nearby restaurant. We decided to make this a real break: We planned to feast without guilt. "On a girl getaway, there are no calories!" Linda joked. Then my friends started complaining about their bodies. Can we women ever get together without complaining about our thighs, waists, or that last miserable five (okay, twenty-five) pounds?

In this posse of girls, I was Sporty Spice. I suggested a four-mile hike, and everyone grimaced. "One hill!" I promised. "It's more of a walk than a hike." After getting directions from Roberta, our innkeeper, we headed out in the late afternoon. The Berkshire Hills were quiet and still. For the first mile, I thought about the million things I didn't get done before the trip, and the masochist in my head scolded me: If you were better organized, you wouldn't always be ten paces behind. But as I continued walking, I concentrated instead on the exercise high that was coming on strong.

I love the Berkshires. I see my history in those hills, a younger version of myself. In that tree, I see my first roommate and my first college boyfriend; I see the slope I ran down in my pajamas when I was late to class, the converted barn that serves as the college's photography studio. This is where I changed from girl to woman. And this is where I return when I want to be a girl again.

As we walked, my friends and I floated in and out of conversation. "I think he's my soul mate," Karen said of her then boyfriend, Walter. "And he's so attentive to my daughter. The fact that he cares and he comes to her school events means a lot."

An hour after we set out, it was almost dark and we were nowhere near the inn. A city girl, I underestimated our distance and pace. We worried about finding our way back before it was pitch black, so we began jogging. But the bustier girls among us, suffering without sport bras, cut the jogging short. Just then, we saw the flash of a car's headlights; the first car we'd seen in an hour. None of us said it then, but we later discovered that we were all thinking the same thing: This would be a good time to take up hitchhiking. The car pulled up.

"Have you had enough of an adventure?" We were relieved to see Roberta, our innkeeper. We piled into her car. She apologized for being so protective, but when it was dark and we weren't back, she was worried. "It's the Jewish mother in me," Roberta said.

"Well," said Linda, who is Irish Catholic, "I'm converting."

Roberta figured we'd be cold after our hike through the hills, so a fire awaited us at the inn. We huddled, reading magazines and inhaling chocolate. A half hour earlier, we'd been in a panic; but back at the inn, safe and warm, we devoured goodies and traded stories about the best clothing discounts in the city. Heaven.

"Ever since I saw Sarah Jessica Parker in a poncho," I said, "I've been wanting one in hot pink. When I went to my favorite boutique, guess what was on the rack? A pink poncho in my size!" Everyone turned to me and said, "Wow. Really?" Then I told the best news. "Not only was it a hot pink poncho in my size but it was also fifty percent off!" After a sharp intake of breath, Karen, Linda, and Sarah said, in unison, "Oooh." We threw our heads back and cackled. Boys tell ghost stories when they gather around a fire. But girls? We tell shopping stories.

An hour later, at eight, we sat across the table from one another at John Andrews, a nearby restaurant. Before our trip, I asked everyone to write down five things she was proud of having done in the past year, five dreams she had for the coming year, and five things she would do if money were no object and no one would laugh. Sarah, the artist, was proud of "knowing when to quit my job and actually going through with it. But this next one is goofy." After some coaxing, Sarah said she was also proud of "maintaining a great relationship" with her fiancé. We assured her it wasn't silly or small.

Karen, who dropped out of college when she became pregnant, was proud of recently returning to school. We all cheered. She planned to get her bachelor's and law degrees. Earlier Linda joked, "It would be a lot easier if you'd asked for a list of failures. I remember my failures." But even with last year's challenges, she won her first Emmy for a documentary on Italian-Americans. Sometimes, I want to shake her and the others for being so self-critical. But I'm the same way. I gloss over my successes and dwell on what I perceive as failures.

"Nine years ago, I left an abusive relationship with the father of my twins," Linda said as our waitress put pasta and steaks before us. "I had no money. I had to live with friends." We were so shocked by Linda's revelation—she hadn't told any of us about this—that none of us touched our food. Linda eased the awkwardness by dropping into a Blanche DuBois impersonation, saying how much she had "depended on the kindness of strangers," then she told us how buying her first home that year had made her feel. "I got the bottom-floor condo, not facing the water, and it's the smallest one—but it's mine. Giving my girls a real home made me feel as though I'd made it." She continued: "When you asked me what I'm proud of, I thought I'd have to make up something. But I am a survivor. That's the gift I can give my twins—what it means to face an obstacle and win."

When Karen said she couldn't come up with anything else she's proud of, I reminded her of all she does for her daughter. "I'm supposed to do that," she said, shrugging. We all dissented. Karen is a loving, dedicated mom whose daughter is an A student and a dancer who has performed across the country. "You have to be proud of yourself; you're doing this by yourself," Linda said. "God forbid something happens to us. Our kids will be alone." We broke into tears.

The subject of what we're proud of was long behind us before I felt comfortable enough to open up. "One of the things I'm proud of this year is choosing to stay single instead of dating guys who make me feel bad about myself," I said. Everyone applauded. When I announced that I'd won a fellowship to study in Japan, my friends toasted me. I often keep my good news to myself because I fear others will think I'm bragging. But that evening, Karen, Sarah, and Linda provided a space in which I felt safe enough to speak. When I am insecure or self-critical, my friends are both mirrors and crystal balls. They reflect all the good things about me I cannot see, and they assure me that my future is as bright as I want it to be.

I climbed into bed on Saturday night feeling like I rarely do—content. Instead of riffling through my past or agonizing about what's ahead, I was able to be still, for a moment, in the present.

The next day we ate lunch at a pizzeria. Karen told us how she recently had a session with a fortune-teller who had called out to her. "I never stop for those people," Karen said, "but she surprised me by saying that I had just returned from Miami, which was true."

"What did you ask her?" I wondered.

"About my job, my relationship, my daughter, going back to school. The more I asked, the more way-out her answers were. I was disappointed when I realized she was a fake. I guess I wanted someone to tell me I'm doing the right things."

I knew what Karen meant. I think of the women I admire: Julie Taymor, who won a Tony for directing Broadway's *The Lion King*; Pulitzer Prize–winner Toni Morrison; Judith Jamison, artistic director of the Alvin Ailey American Dance Theater. These women are twenty to thirty years older than I am, and I want to ask them, "How do I get from here to where you are?" I want a thirty-year blueprint, and there is none. I'm impatient, and what I fear most is that I'll make a mistake. There is a quote by Sophia Loren that hangs on my bathroom mirror: "Mistakes are part of the dues one pays for a full life." I read it every day and understand it, but only in my head.

As we parted, we hugged and promised to re-gather at year's end. "You can do it!" Linda told Karen about returning to school. "You'll find the work that inspires you," I assured Sarah. Linda promised to introduce me to her cute guy friend, who I had a crush on. Three hours later, I took the New York City exit off the freeway. I was sure my voice mail and e-mail were overflowing. And my cell phone was already ringing. But I ignored it all, went home, turned off the phone, lit a scented candle, and drew a bubble bath.

Not until later did I realize that our retreat had been the authentic success I'd been looking for, because it prompted me to ask myself some hard questions: Am I living the life I want to live? Does my work matter? What is my purpose? These questions are scary (okay, terrifying) because the answers might mean making huge changes.

But having the courage to examine my life, however it looks that day, is the way to real meaning. I could have everything I love in my friends' lives—a wonderful fiancé, a beautiful daughter, a new condo, even an Emmy—but without my asking the hard questions, fulfillment would elude me. Then there are the smaller delights that mean success: allowing others to compliment me, enjoying a deep-down belly laugh, soaking in a bubble bath. Success surely means surrounding myself with loving people who bring me joy.

When I can't find a group to experience joy with, a buddy and a convertible will do. So when I received an assignment to drive around southern Baja California, with a good friend and a new convertible, I knew what to do. I have a confession to make. When it comes to cars, I'm like a fifty-year-old man in a midlife crisis. Don't talk to me about safety. Don't talk to me about practical. And since the assignment put me in a new sports car, everything was perfect. The car was happening: silver, sporty, sleek. I had a wardrobe to match and CDs hot enough to make the pavement sizzle.

The only problem was that the drive itself consisted of long stretches of desert, without a single cute guy in sight. This provoked a philosophical dilemma, akin to the question whether a tree falling in a forest makes a sound if no one is around to hear it—namely, if I'm a total babe in a cute car with nobody but cacti to flirt with, am I still a total babe? I decided it was worth the trip just to find out.

First, I needed a partner in crime. The schedule I had in mind went like this: wake up, loll about in the pool until noon, break the speed laws in six Mexican counties, and pray that I don't get arrested. What I needed for the trip was a homegirl, someone to play Thelma to my Louise. Someone who'd let me drive, tolerate my singing, and not whine, "But you always get to be Louise!"

The first call I made was to my friend Jennifer. Jen just had a baby, so she had no free time whatsoever. She also lived in California (at the time, I was living in New York) so we saw each other far too little. I got her answering machine and left a message to the effect of, "Got a great assignment. Driving trip in Baja. Babe-mobile convertible. Too bad you have a newborn infant. Wanted you to come." Then I went away on a business trip. Checking my voice mail from Spain, I got the following message. "Booked ticket. Will miss the kid, but will get over it. See you in Baja."

Our first stop in Baja was the Las Ventanas al Paraíso resort in San José del Cabo. It had been my dream to stay there ever since I saw a picture of it on the cover of *Travel +*

Leisure. There had been many a day of visualizing myself floating in the famous rimless pool or dozing in a hammock on the white-sand beach that kept me from going postal when work was hell. We checked into the hotel, and it was heaven. Our room was huge, with hand-set mosaic floors, a private pool, and high, beamed ceilings. Jen was happy to find a complimentary bottle of smooth tequila in the room. I ordered up a kiwi margarita from room service. Forget driving Baja; we may never leave the hotel.

The next morning we tore ourselves away from Las Ventanas to take the Spyder for a quick spin around Cabo San Lucas. We attracted the requisite amount of attention. Mission accomplished—it was a total babe-mobile. But it was also a hundred degrees outside, and the Las Ventanas pool was calling. We went back to the hotel for lunch and a swim. Check-out time is noon, but neither of us wanted to leave the beloved pool. So I got out and called my main man, Mañuel, at the front desk. "Can we stay until one P.M.?" He said yes.

An hour later, we were still in the pool. "Call him back," Jen said. "No, I called last time," I said, trying to float backward. "Oh, all right," Jen said. Two seconds later, she returned triumphant. "He said two o'clock is fine!" Then, because Jen and I together are the silliest girls you'll ever meet, we started to do a victory dance in the pool. We got a drink at the swim-up bar. I was doing the doggie paddle and complaining about my suit not being babe-worthy when I heard this voice say, "No, you're wrong. You look great in that suit. I was just thinking I should get one like it." I turn around and saw that the woman speaking was Brooke Shields. Needless to say, I was stoked.

At 2:30, we got into the car and started driving toward Cabo San Lucas, land of chaos and countless cheesy restaurants and nightclubs. We stopped just long enough to buy Jen a hat and then hit the road again. Our plan was to drive to the capital city of La Paz, spend the night, and drive back to Las Ventanas the next day. It was only a three-hour haul. Route 1 would have been faster, but we took the more scenic Route 19, which has intermittent vistas of the ocean.

We were heading first for Todos Santos, an artist community halfway to La Paz, where we thought we'd stop for an early supper. But for the good two hours it took to get there, the entire world melted away. There was a kind of reassuring sameness about driving through the desert. The Spyder is shaped like a silver bullet and handled the hills like a dream. Although there were stretches of road that just begged me to rev up to ninety miles per hour, mostly I resisted the temptation because the views—and the ride—were too sweet to be rushed. I had always thought of the desert as one brown blur, but Baja is colorful: green cacti, rock formations in shades of brown and black, desert flowers we couldn't name, vivid altars built to honor those who have died along these roads.

Jen and I were so enamored of the scenery that we kept pulling over to take pictures of each other: She posed with the cacti. I posed with the cacti. She posed with the car. I posed with the car. In between our photo shoots, Jen caught me up on her life, telling me stories about her husband, her baby, her work at the Museum of Contemporary Art. I told her stories about my travels, my dating life, my new job.

Then there was the music. Since she was driving shotgun, Jen was the DJ, and she had burned a special "Baja Mix" CD for our trip. The minute I heard Michael Jackson, I started singing. Jen joined in. We were both awful, but the car was our own private karaoke booth. Except it wasn't. We elicited more than a few stares from other drivers when we started singing Luscious Jackson's "Strongman" at the top of our lungs. Too bad.

At that point it was five P.M. and we were starving. We headed to Café Sante Fe, the Spago of Todos Santos, which has a beautiful garden of hibiscus, bougainvillea, and papaya trees. I was a little disappointed to learn that the menu was Italian instead of Mexican, but the pasta was delicious, the bread was fresh, and I was in love with the portraits of Frida Kahlo that the owner had commissioned from local artists. An hour later, we set out to tour the town's galleries, of which there are many, including the renowned Galería Todos Santos and Galería Santa Fe. But as we strolled down the cobblestone streets, my urge to shop began to battle with my need for speed. How badly did I want a gilded Virgin of Guadalupe or a Frida-portrait mirror? "What do you want to do?" I asked Jen. She gave a sheepish grin. "I really just want to get back to the car." Minutes later, we had the top down and Madonna pumping. We sang "Ray of Light" all the way out of Todos Santos.

In La Paz, we pulled into the Posada Santa Fe, a bed-and-breakfast on the waterfront. Southern Baja, from Las Ventanas's high-end corridor to the party-hearty flavor of Cabo San Lucas, is unmistakably touristy; La Paz feels more like a real Mexican city. In fact, with the exception of mirrors, you can pass hours without seeing a gringo—to my mind, a good thing. We had a lovely dinner at El Zarape, which specializes in seafood, and then went for a walk along the waterfront. Everywhere we turned there were children, families, and couples. Unlike in downtown Cabo San Lucas, where you can't walk two blocks without someone handing you a flier for a restaurant or hotel or disco, in La Paz no one tried to sell us anything. We stared out at the ocean, eating ice cream cones bought from a local vendor. Home felt a million miles away.

The next day, the drive back to Los Cabos was just as

thrilling. We sang along to Mary J. Blige and Aretha Franklin, ate shrimp tacos until we were about to bust. I drove Jen to the airport, where she went over her life plan for me and reassured me that children and wedded bliss were in my future. In the meantime, she said I must do my best to seduce one of the guys we met at Las Ventanas. "Do it for me," she said mischievously. "I'm married. I can't." Instead, I took the car out for one more spin. Finally, I gave in to my impulse to race the sporty model. The car surged to eighty miles per hour with no hesitation. I inched up to eighty-nine, with the full view of the ocean to my left and the desert to my right. I'm no Thelma or Louise, and in less than a day I'd be home and back at work, but for the next few hours, the convertible was mine. Like someone sitting through a favorite movie twice, I was tempted to gun it up to La Paz one more time. Anything to keep on driving.

If going away with friends is a journey inward, then traveling with strangers is a kick in the comfort-zone pants. I was living and studying in Japan when I received an intriguing e-mail from my *compañera* and fellow writer Angie Cruz. It was an invitation to apply for a two-week fellowship in Spain for Jovenes Líderes Hispanos. The Spanish Embassy was looking for bright young Latina and Latino achievers between the ages of twenty-eight and thirty-eight to gather for a conference. We would spend our days with Spain's top minds in seminars on politics, business, new media, the economy, and culture. We would also get to take sightseeing trips to the coast and Madrid. Candidates had to be fluent in Spanish because no English would be spoken in the programs. All expenses would be paid.

The chance to return to Spain, with the Spanish Embassy as my host, seemed like a dream made real. The chance to travel *anywhere*, all expenses paid, was a complete blessing. I sent the e-mail to my friend John Leland, a senior writer at the *New York Times,* with a note that said, "Wouldn't this be cool? If I apply, would you write me a recommendation?" Then I promptly forgot about it.

Luckily for me, John did not forget. He wrote me a recommendation and sent it in to the Spanish Embassy. They called me and asked me for the rest of my application and then, a miracle. I was accepted into the program. Immediately, a kind of fifth-grade panic set in. What if the other kids didn't like me? The truth is, outside of my family, I don't have a ton of Latino friends—and it *is* for lack of trying. I hate having to explain that, even though my name is Chambers and I'm black, I'm also Latina. I hate playing "How Latin Are You?," measuring fluency and accents against birthplace and birthrights.

I've written two popular children's books featuring young Latina girls, but even on book tour, I felt a chill from the community. At one Hispanic Book Fair, I arrived and asked for the coordinator. A suspicious-looking woman told me she was very busy. I pointed to the gigantic poster on the wall advertising my book and explaining that I was the author of *Marisol and Magdalena*. The woman gave me the once over and took me to a back room to wait. I waited and waited for four hours. Then they told me that they didn't have that many copies of my book and it didn't make sense for me to read after all. The implication being that I didn't look Latina and so I might as well go home. Did I mention I had taken a three-hour flight to get there? I wanted to go to Spain, but I worried about two weeks of getting dissed by a high-profile assortment of *jovenes líderes hispanos*.

What happened on that trip couldn't have been a more different truth. From the start, the group bonded and I never felt more included. The first night, a bunch of us went salsa dancing and I won't lie—my moves leave something to be desired. One of the guys just took me by the hand and said, "It's okay, *mami*. You've just got a little too much hip-hop in your paseo. It's not Jay-Z, okay? You

don't bounce with me, you glide with me." The men—
David, Jeffrey, Olveen, Vincente, and the others—were all
absolute *caballeros*. It was like being at a wedding with all
your cute cousins. They all took turns dancing with the
girls and never let any *chica* become the wallflower. For
two weeks straight, we danced every night. And when we
weren't too hung over, Jaime, Joe, and I went jogging. We
spent the first week at the University of Santander, housed
in a beautiful old castle on the northern coast. Some of
my happiest memories of that summer are of getting up
early with the guys and jogging along the ocean as the
waves broke on the rocks.

The women were even more incredible. AnaMary
had done a religious pilgrimage through Spain. Patricia
had lobbied on Capitol Hill on behalf of bilingual education—and also told the best jokes. My roommate, Angela,
was an incredibly sophisticated Argentine woman. She
had such great style—classic shift dresses, beautiful simple jewelry—she reminded me of a Latina Jackie O. As a
Latina so fair, she could be American or Italian. Angela is
exactly the type of person I used to be intimidated by. But
she couldn't have been warmer. She's a writer for the
Smithsonian, so we shared a passion for art and literature.

I learned so much from Angela that summer, and
most important was her ability to put people at ease. Sitting at a dinner table, she always managed to bring even

the shyest person into the conversation. "What was your happiest Christmas?" she would ask. "What was your worst New Year?" Instantly, the whole group would be involved in an entertaining conversation. Angela was like the aunt that always looked out for the underdog. Even when divisions arose in the group, she always brought people together. In the months since I met Angela, I've made a concerted effort to emulate her graciousness. Now, at a party or a meeting, I pay more attention to those who are being left out and try to bring them into the fold.

We joked about our Spanish hosts being *conquistadores* confronted by the chickens who've come home to roost. We spent long evenings eating paella and drinking *tinto,* and sharing the stories of our lives. We were Peruvian, Columbian, Cuban, Mexican, Panamanian, Argentine, and Puerto Rican. We were—as *Generación Ñ*—incredibly diverse but remarkably alike. We were from different countries, but we could all joke about our relatives' plastic-covered furniture and our *abuelos'* plastic-covered memories.

I was embarrassed at first about my gringo accent, but Felipe, our group leader, helped me become more confident about speaking out loud. Sometimes, in the midst of a heavy political conversation, I would raise my hand and say, "Sorry, I've got to speak in English" because I just couldn't express certain complex ideas in Spanish. But not long after, others followed suit. The rule was that we were to speak Spanish all the time, but we were young Latinos, not *madrileños.* Our collective native tongue was Spanglish.

One afternoon on a bus trip to Cervantes's birthplace, I looked around the bus at the faces of my new friends and I felt what I so rarely feel in the United States—an incredible sense of belonging. I found myself wishing that I could spend all my time with people like this: young, smart Latinos of all different backgrounds, who were open-minded, passionate about our people but laid-back enough to have a good time. If this bus were a neighborhood, I thought, this is where I'd want to live.

I realized that on a deeper level, this trip was a reminder that even when I'm separated from my culture for swaths of time, it is always waiting—like a lover, like an old friend—for me to reconnect. Dancing to merengue hits in Madrid, climbing the Picos de Europa, crossing myself as I entered each ancient cathedral, my spirit would sing. The Spanglish, the *baile,* the sweet gestures of my new friends were all touchstones to my Latina self, a bridge back to the place where—even with my hip-hop salsa moves, my Flatbush Avenue accent, and my dark skin—I belong.

Conclusion: Wish Well

ONE OF MY MOST VIVID MEMORIES OF MY COLLEGE freshman orientation took place in the evening as I had gathered with a group of other students around a fire in the woods. My alma mater has a distinctly hippie bent and even though this was the 1980s, someone was wearing tie-dye and someone had brought a guitar—and, although I was too naive to know it, I am certain that more than a few people were high. There was music and talking, lots of political talk about every kind of "ism" from socialism to Marxism and racism and sexism and feminism. And, oh yeah, homophobia too—not technically an ism, but a concern of politicized college kids all the same. I remember being wowed that everyone was so serious, and I wasn't jaded enough to see that this kind of seriousness was, in and of itself a pose. All I could think was, "Thank God I'm not in high school anymore." Then a beautiful young man, a sophomore, with shoulder-length blond hair that he wore in a ponytail, announced that he was going to read a poem. Every girl around the fire began to sweat, just a little. Then the sophomore read, from memory, T. S. Eliot's "The Love Song of J. Alfred Prufrock." It didn't matter that this was a poem that we all had read in high school. By the time he got to the lines "In the room the women come and go / Talking of Michelangelo," we were beside ourselves with lust and love and admiration. Which, of course, was the desired effect.

"In his day, he said, students were grounded in spelling and had learned poetry and the Bible by heart," A. S. Byatt writes in *Possession.* "An odd phrase, by heart, he would add, as though poems were stored in the bloodstream." I do not have poems stored in my bloodstream. What I am good at remembering are phone numbers. I know, of course, all of my husband's phone numbers. I also have memorized my parents', my brother's, my nieces' and nephews' and my in-laws'. In addition, I can remember, at any given time, the phone numbers of twenty or so of my closest friends and relatives. From time to time, random phone numbers pop up: the phone number of a friend at a job where she no longer works, my aunt's old Brooklyn phone number. I am pretty good with addresses and zip codes, I have quite a few of those memorized. Which strikes me as strange, seeing as I am not good at math. But I am grateful for my gifts, regardless how minuscule or random.

One day, I would like to learn a poem by heart. The one that I am closest to memorizing is "One Art" by Elizabeth Bishop. I first read this poem when I was seventeen years old and in the nearly twenty years since, it has never failed to inspire me. At my darkest moments, the lines of the poem come back to me, jovial and singsong and yet remarkably profound. It is a poem about losing and yet every time I read it, it fills me up.

ONE ART

Elizabeth Bishop

The art of losing isn't hard to master;
So many things seem filled with the intent
To be lost, that their loss is no disaster.

Lose something every day. Accept the fluster
Of lost door keys, the hour badly spent.
The art of losing isn't hard to master.

Then practice losing farther, losing faster:
Places and names and where it was you meant
To travel. None of these will bring disaster.

I lost my mother's watch. And look! My last
Next to last, of three loved houses went
The art of losing isn't hard to master.

I lost two cities, lovely ones. And vaster,
Some realms I owned, two rivers, a continent.
I miss them, but it wasn't a disaster.

Even losing you (the joking voice, a gesture
I love) I shan't have lied. It's evident
The art of losing's not too hard to master

Though it may look like (Write it) like disaster.

To me, this poem is the very spirit of the joy of doing things badly. "Practice losing farther, losing faster," I tell myself when an editor calls to say that she doesn't like my article and is paying me only the 25 percent kill fee. "Lose something every day, accept the fluster," I tell myself when I'm running late for work and I've been up since six A.M. but somehow it's managed to morph into 8:55 A.M. and I am dashing for the front door. And what I most want to commit to memory, to have pulsing through my bloodstream when I learn this poem "by heart" is the reminder that no loss, no matter what it feels like, is truly a disaster.

In this self-help culture, I think it is nearly impossible to separate the notion of self-improvement from the faulty notion that we are all so screwed up that we are in desperate need of improving. We can and should do what we can to make our lives easier. I have finally carved out the time to put some self-care tools in place. At work, I keep a drawer stocked with everything that I might need: from an aromatherapy candle to personal items like sanitary napkins and Advil. I keep some healthy snacks on hand in case I don't get to have breakfast before I leave home. And I keep some small treats, such as little scented towelettes from Paris. I've learned that my twice weekly run is better when I wake up in the morning and play some inspirational music instead of squeezing in a phone call or checking e-mail before I work out. "I want you to win," Connie Bennett always tells my African dance class. "I'm setting this up so it's as easy as possible for you to feel good." When I'm happiest, I'm being that gentle and careful with myself.

At the same time, sometimes I grow tired of feeling as if my life were a house constantly under renovation. I long to feel comfortable in my own skin. I know I'm not alone in this. I was watching *Comedian,* a documentary about Jerry Seinfeld's return to the comedy circuit after the massive success of his television show. Jerry had retired all of his old material and was hitting the road with all new jokes. The documentary was a revelation, absolutely inspiring, in the way that it showed this man who seemed to have everything: wealth, fame, and the love of the critics. But here he was, choosing the more difficult journey, to keep going creatively. Moreover, he was experiencing real vulnerability and fear. "It's so fucking hard to get comfortable, it just comes and goes," Seinfeld said. "There are just little glimpses, little moments when I feel like myself and I feel comfortable. The rest of it, I'm like in my father's suit with huge sleeves and legs and I'm thinking, 'What am I wearing? What am I doing here?' "

What are we doing here? Several years ago, I read an article in a women's magazine about all the things that you need to let go of when you turn thirty. Some of the advice I related to: I too was beginning to weary of the credit card shopping sprees (and the repercussions therein) and the allure of the bad boy was wearing thin. But the one thing that I could not give up, the one twenty-something dream on the list that I clung to was the idea that one day I would learn to speak French and one day I would live in Paris.

Talk about the joy of doing things badly. The American girl who dreams of living in Paris is probably the most wholly unoriginal idea going. For years, I avoided even visiting Paris, convinced that it would be as stereotypical as a book of picture postcards. Then finally, I went. And I did not want to leave. The cafés and the markets and the churches and the squares were all as they appeared in films and that, in and of itself, was a thrill. What's wrong with the stereotype, if the stereotype is as glorious as the Tuilleries, the Eiffel Tower, the shops on the Boulevard Saint-Germain. Whereas once Paris had been a haven for African-Americans, more recently France has struggled with its identity as the Arabs and Africans who live in the city suburbs struggle for visibility and power. To me, that type of struggle makes the city even more interesting. I can give up many unrealistic hopes and dreams: Maybe I will never learn to play an instrument or earn a master's degree and I'm more than confident that I will never weigh what I did when I graduated from college. But I cannot, will not give up on Paris.

I've been studying French for over a year now, and

while I did Jane Austen Thursdays for only three months, I do not want to stop studying French. I'm not sure what to do about my upcoming birthday. The idea behind the Birthday Passions was to do one thing a year with no goals of completion. When I started the Birthday Passions I pictured myself flitting from hobby to hobby: from Jane Austen to French to swimming to a year spent teaching myself how to make Korean barbecue. But I want to keep up my French. If I add another Birthday Passion to the mix, will I just be falling back into the depths of over-achieving? Or is it simply that my play life—the time I spend running and studying French and doing water aerobics—is asserting itself, growing stronger and more expansive and demanding to be taken as seriously as my work life?

Throughout my life, one constant has been my passion for learning languages. It is true that I had certain advantages as the daughter of immigrants. But my father ran a strict, "You're in America, speak English" household. So to me, Spanish, my parents' tongue, was covert, secret, mysterious, a language I eventually learned in school. In fifth grade, I studied French. In seventh grade, I began what would be eight years of diligent Spanish lessons. In tenth grade, I studied German. In college, I studied Russian. The year I turned thirty, I began Japanese.

I am old enough to know that I will probably never

be the urbane sophisticate that I once dreamed of being—Katharine Hepburn with a heavy-duty arsenal of Berlitz. I will probably never be a diplomat. I'm fairly confident that I will never be a war photographer like my once-upon-a-time idol Margaret Bourke-White. Sometimes I wonder if listening to language tapes in the car is really worth it for the two weeks a year I manage to spend abroad most years. But I know that the pleasure of speaking languages is less about the time I spend abroad than the way I live my life. The pleasure of watching a Pedro Almodóvar movie in Spanish or catching a raunchy talk show in Spanish on Univision. The warm familiarity of being in a Japanese noodle shop in New York and ordering *onigiri, ramen,* and *ume shu.*

"My father always said that the most important thing in life is to remain interested," Anjelica Huston once said. "I'm very rarely bored. I like to observe the human condition." Learning languages, along with my love of travel, is my way of extracting my head from my navel and connecting to the world outside of my own life, experience, and perspective.

There's a funny scene in the latest series of *Absolutely Fabulous* when hapless fashion wannabe Edina, takes her conservative daughter Saffy, to Paris. She nearly faints when she hears Saffy order a meal in flawless French. "You should speak French more often," Edina says, impressed.

"Everything you say sounds interesting in French." I think in some ways, I am both the mother and daughter in that skit. I am wise enough, as the daughter is, to know that ordering a meal in French will never impress a Parisian. But I am as hapless and provincial as the mother, in that I do believe that when I am speaking a foreign language, I am somehow more interesting. It has been this way, since I was ten years old. The two and two quarters languages that I speak (English, Spanish, a smattering of Japanese, a little bit of French) impresses no one but myself. But in a life rampant with insecurity, I believe that impressing myself, challenging myself with language, is a very fine thing.

There is so much legend and lore about wishes. If you tell someone your wish, it won't come true. If you want something too badly, you won't get it. At the same time, be careful what you wish for, you may get it. The legend of the genie in the bottle is that you get only three wishes, so you best wish well. I like to believe that wishes are like prayers—infinite and powerful and open to revision.

All of my adult life I have had a passion for what I call OPC, other people's children. What I think about when I remember my twenties is being at the house of my friends Jeff and Jenny late on Christmas Eve and writing Santa's letter, because we knew that their daughter, Lily, would not recognize my handwriting. I remember having a fridge that always contained two things: a bottle of champagne in case I had romantic company and a roll of cookie dough in case one of my pals dropped by with their kids. I have a pretty decent shoe collection: Gucci, Jimmy Choo, Sigerson Morrison. But my collection of picture books is devastating. I can do story time with the best of them. I love introducing my nieces and nephews and kid friends to my favorite books, jump rope tricks, and rhymes. But more than that, I try to have my own relationship with the children in my life. I write them letters. I call them up for play dates.

I was six when I moved for the first time, away from my dearest friend in England, where we had lived since I was a toddler. We moved again when I was seven. Again, when I was ten. Again, when I was thirteen. Again, at fourteen, at fifteen, at sixteen. Because I have turned self-flagellation into a kind of beaux arts, I have long told myself that my lack of childhood friends is yet another sign of my own unworthiness. Now that I have friendships with people the ages I once was, I know that constant moving is hard on children. If I do not know that many people from when I was young, it is because it is hard for children to stay in touch. My Polaroid camera has become my best friend. Especially when I write our nieces, Magdalena and Sophia. I like to send them funny pictures of my husband: with a stalk of celery "growing" out of his hair, balancing a jar of peanut butter on his head. The distance forces me to use my imagination. Back then, as is true for the here and now, I do my best. Some people are in your life for a reason, a season, or a lifetime, I tell myself, quoting the words I first read in Iyanla Vanzant's *Acts of Faith*. It is as true for the young people in my life as it is of ex-boyfriends, old college roommates, former neighbors, colleagues, and friends. But it is the children I know who have taught me how to be in the moment of a relationship. Maybe one day they'll forget how we were pals when they were little, it is likely they may not remember trips to the petting zoos, or the time we baked Christmas cookies. But *I* remember, and I have grown through these experiences. Back when I was dating, crying into pay phones on street corners and nursing heartbreak like a barfly nursing cocktails, I wish I had known that time is no measure of value. I know now, because the children in my life have taught me that love does not have to last forever to be real.

"It takes a village to raise a child" was first an African proverb, then the title of a book by Hillary Clinton, but on a day-to-day basis, what does that actually mean? I think it means that you show up for the children that you know, as often and as well as you can. So I go to dance recitals and school plays and at Christmas, when my husband and I throw our annual tree-trimming party, I try to go above and beyond—like the time I spent all day making a lopsided gingerbread house that the kids who came to the party could decorate.

Over the past few years, as I've gotten into my thirties, I've upped the ante for the OPC in my life. Realizing that my young relatives were so worn out from opening presents on Christmas Day that they couldn't care less what was in box number thirty-nine, I pulled back on my present giving. This was tough. Presents are where I go into full Auntie Mame mode and Auntie Mame mode makes me happy. It took me six months, for example, to find a Hawaiian tiki hut/lemonade stand (and a pair of matching grass skirts) to ship to my nieces in Philadelphia. The year before, I had given my nephews a laptop computer.

But realizing that the kids in my life actually didn't need more stuff, I began to open 529 savings funds for their college education. This turned out to be surprisingly easy—and fairly affordable. With a minimum $25 monthly contribution, I could set up an automatic withdrawal from my bank account. After a while, that $50 or $75 didn't hurt at all. It was like an additional electric bill or phone bill. And when I begin to worry that I am the most useless person on the planet, I take out a calculator and I start to add up what that money will be, at an average 7 percent return rate, when my nieces and nephews turn eighteen. And I feel good. I feel more than good. I feel Auntie Mame fabulous! Because I'm not a rich woman, and I can't do 529 funds for every young relative in my family, I've also set up Upromise accounts for some of the other kids in my life. This is easy, I went to Upromise.com, registered my credit cards, and a percentage of everything I spend on things like gas and restaurants and groceries, goes into these accounts. It's not as lucrative as the 529, but I estimate that by the time the kids get to college, there will be two or three thousand in each account: enough to help with books or dorm fees or meals.

For the past few years, I've also taken on summers with my nephews. One year, I sent my nephew Frederick to football camp at the University of Pennsylvania. He comes from a really rough neighborhood, and at the time, he was thirteen and already getting in trouble with gangs. He's a talented football player, hence the nature of the camp; but more than anything I wanted him to get a glimpse of college life. I loved driving him up to the Penn dorms, setting up his room, seeing him take in campus life for the first time. The summer after that, I sent Frederick's brother, Jesse, to mountain biking camp in New Hampshire. Again, I was looking for an experience that wouldn't make Jesse feel like a Fresh Air Fund kid; yet I wanted him to get a glimpse of a different life, and it seemed like mountain biking in the great outdoors would be a great move. We were too late to qualify for any type of financial aid (most camps offer some sort of scholarship), but when I explained the situation, the camp director, Fiona, threw in the bike and equipment rental for free. Jesse had a blast and spent two weeks biking down ski trails and riding through mud; he also learned how to pitch a tent and surf. And I became the coolest aunt ever. Mission accomplished.

This past summer, Jesse, who was twelve, came to stay with us for seven weeks. He took a forensics science class in the morning (CSI: Junior High) and a School of Rock course in the afternoon, where he built on the drum lessons he had been taking the previous year. It's one thing to write checks, drive them to and from the airport or train station, but having someone come and live with us for the summer took things to another level. It was summer, but Jesse had school work to do and book reports to write. Jason and I had to learn to how to be disciplinarians, and we also had to learn how to manage his social schedule. Play dates. The first day I had two twelve-year-old boys running up and down my house, I thought I was going to lose my mind. Then came the day when I had four twelve-year-old boys running up and through the house, and I realized I had no mind left to lose. And that was more than okay. I loved it.

My husband and I developed a routine that I imagine will serve us well one day if, when, we have kids of our own. I got up at six and tried to get in some exercise. I came home, showered, and my husband left for work. I woke up Jesse and walked him to school, then hightailed it to my own office. My husband had changed his hours to 8 A.M. until 4 P.M. for the summer. So when Jesse got out of school at three, he only had an hour until Jason got home. Jesse and Jason got supper ready. Then I came home, and we all hung out. There were hard moments: times when Jesse let us know, for all intents and purposes, that we were not his parents and we could rot in Hell for all he cared. There were doors slammed and more than a few tears. Both Jason and I were trying to get a feel for the boundaries. Being an aunt and uncle is not the same as being a mother and father. How much authority could we assert? How much of Jesse's routine could we rightfully change? What would help him be more disciplined and do better at school when he went home? And what was just too confusing and too much of a disconnect from what he already knew? It was tough. But in the end we decided we could do only what real parents actually do: wing it and pray that when we got it wrong, we weren't doing irreparable damage.

I'm guessing we didn't, because the last night Jesse was with us, he was invited to a party where all the cool kids he had met over the summer were going to be hanging out. We had planned to take him out to dinner and to hear some jazz (Jesse is an aspiring drummer), but we let him decide what he wanted to do. Jesse said what he really wanted to do was make dinner at home and for all of us to play Monopoly. Just when we were about to set the table for dinner, the phone rang. It was Jesse's friend calling from the party. Jesse said, "Yeah. It sounds great. But you know it's my last night, and I think my aunt and uncle need some quality time."

After Jesse left, Jason and I had the conversation we have had a hundred zillion times. What are we going to do with our own lives? We would like to have a family, and we would really like to adopt. But our nieces and nephews are getting older. Each year, these kids become more independent and interesting. We would love to have every summer be like the summer we spent with Jesse. I have fantasies of taking my nieces to Paris and my nephews to Tokyo, of showing them all the places I've been and loved. I would like to be able to help even more with college and graduate school, to help offset the cost of a low-paying, but worthy, summer internship, and to have our bank account be an extension of their parents'.

Sometimes Jason and I think, "Why should we bother reaching into the ether, for children we do not know who might be wretched" when there already is this group of a half dozen children that have staked their claim in our world, that we know and love and adore. Isn't it selfish of us to make the world more crowded when we can use what we have to make life easier and more adventurous for the children in our lives? Again and again, we get stuck at the same place. We love our friends' kids. We love our nieces and nephews. And being the relief pitcher parent is chock-full of thrills. But the problem with OPC, other people's children, is that you always have to give them back. Then again, a week after my nephew went home for the summer, I walked into his room, converted back to our guest room, and for the first time in months, it did not smell like eau de twelve-year-old boy. I put on a pair of stiletto heels for the first time all summer and I put on a sexy blouse for the first time all summer, and my husband took me to dinner—alone—for the first time all summer. Then the waiter arrived with a lovely bottle of sauvignon blanc, and we raised our glasses to toast to the best part of OPC—freedom.

~

I know it seems like I'm too young to know anything worth sharing about life or love. It is close to twenty years since I began college at the age of sixteen, and I have still managed to stay among the youngest in every job and social group I'm in. I am constantly being told that I am still a baby, that I will have something of value to contribute to the conversation when I am forty, when I have children, when I complete that all-important dissertation in the School of Hard Knocks.

That's the thing, though. I know about hard knocks. Bad things have happened to me. The kind of things that they make TV movies of the week about. The kind of things that have broken strong women into pieces. There are things that I will never tell my closest friends and that I have spent years trying to forget. I love Lemony Snicket's children's book *The Bad Beginning,* because it mirrors my life so tellingly. Things were bad. They got very bad. Then they got worse. In so many ways, it seems like I've been old my whole life. Recently while watching a TV movie, my heart went out to a woman who had practically been a mother to her seven siblings. Her husband wanted to have children, but she wasn't ready. She had been a mother all her life. I grew up under similar circumstances: "the little mother" to my troubled younger sibling, "the little mother" to some of the grown-ups in my family, too.

I once spent several weeks traveling with a woman who was Gwyneth Paltrow beautiful, wealthy, and smart. She spoke five languages, rode horses, and seemed to me to have the kind of life I had always dreamed of. She was not, as you have probably guessed, very happy at all. Her childhood, she told me, had been perfect. Her parents' marriage had been perfect. She felt safe and protected, challenged and intrigued every morning when she opened her eyes and every night when she went to sleep. College and the years afterward had been difficult, she explained. Her life was very comfortable, she told me. She had an engaging job in a laboratory, a lovely husband, close friends, and her beloved family. But everything seemed anticlimatic, she said. I wondered aloud if she'd only thought her childhood had been so flawless, that her parents' marriage was so loving and problem free. She shook her head. It had been perfect, she said, using the p-word for the umpteenth time.

I would give my eyeteeth, a kidney, and a lung, for a happy childhood. I mean happy in the simplest way possible, the way my husband, Jason, describes his childhood with birthday cakes and hours spent playing in the woods. I tell myself I wouldn't need the luxurious childhood of the friend I just described. (Though I think she is not alone, in this country, in her belief that adulthood is anticlimactic.)

It's not just his words but his actions that tell me how very differently my husband and I were raised. He does not flinch when I touch his face. He does not shiver when he sees furniture on the street, he does not start searching for exits in a restaurant when the man at the table next to us begins to bellow. I want what Jason has, not just the confidence with which he carries himself in the world but the past that is the foundation of that confidence. But childhood is fleeting, and since I did not get to choose what my life would be like between birth and the age of eighteen, my adulthood—full of safe spaces, people I can trust, bawling at movies trailers, cotton candy and carousel rides—seems like a pretty good consolation prize to me. It's my deepest belief that if I live to be an old woman, I will leave this earth not as I sometimes still feel, deprived and lacking, but enriched and enchanted, very much ahead.

Sometimes I imagine that I was born an old woman, like those babies who come out of the womb, looking wrinkled and slightly ornery, like seven-pound versions of George Burns. I watch my friends' children cry, and I am amazed and almost envious at their capacity for bursting into tears. I don't remember crying as a child, what I do remember was a constant struggle to blink back the tears. Mine was a household of abuse and terrifying silences. "If you want to cry, I'll give you something to cry about" was a popular and not hollow refrain. So it did not matter if I fell, or if I had a hundred and three fever, or if someone called me a name, I did not cry. I cry now, all the time. It doesn't take a maudlin movie for me to let loose the waterworks, I cry upon ripping open a birthday card, at movie trailers, at long-distance telephone commercials.

My husband likes to time it, like an anesthesiologist counting a patient out to oblivion, thirty, twenty-nine, twenty-eight, tears . . ." he says laughing. Most of my friends laugh, but I know that there is an immense freedom in the way I cry now. I sometimes believe that I am not growing older. I am growing younger; younger and older at the same time. Creating spaces in my adult life to be the child I never could be.

One does not need to have been abused to feel as if they had been born old. There are so many of us, we could start a movement. We are the daughters of beauty queens whose mothers could never relinquish being the center of attention. We are the relatives of alcoholics and drug abusers, the Co-Dependent No More generation. We are men and women who were raised by grandparents, brought up in old people's houses, and are most comfortable with old people's ways. Some of us were superintelligent: isolated, aged by our bookishness. Others among us have always been too gifted or too spiritual for our age. We can guess that Picasso, Frida Kahlo, and Romare Bearden were all born old; and we can pretty much assume that Mother Teresa, John Coltrane, and Eleanor Roosevelt were born old, too. Lest we think this is some self-indulgent by-product of too much therapy, we know our condition is ancient. Almost every culture has a term for the children they call old souls.

My point is that we know who we are, and there are really only two choices. We can rail against stolen childhoods and all that was lost, spending our lives wallowing in resentment. Or we can carve out spaces in our adult lives for all that we missed, jelling the pieces of our child-like indulgences and our hard-won maturity together like the black-and-white apostrophes that make the yin/yang symbol. The latter has been my choice. And while it's true that I am still so young, that I am in so many ways still a baby, I believe that life has not offered me the short end of the stick. I have become very good at babying myself, and what's more, I do it on a thirty-something's allowance. So I go to the teenage girl store Delia and I buy Kermit and Miss Piggy T-shirts on sale. Moreover I wear them, every chance I get. Matter of fact, as I write these words, I'm wearing my favorite Kermit T. Because I rarely had a lunchbox as a kid—and sometimes, as in the most abusive household I lived in, I was not allowed to eat at all—I buy myself lunchboxes and I fill them with photos and letters from people I love. I swing in playgrounds, and I'm not embarrassed to stand and wait until some uppity elementary-school kid finishes his turn and gets off.

I am not actually a big candy eater, but when I do buy candy, I go whole hog. Swaths of pink cotton candy. Milky Ways. Twizzlers. Gummi Bears. Sour worms. Everything I could put a price to at the age of ten, but could never own.

There is more. Act II, scene 2, of my childhood includes jumping double Dutch in my high heels. I go to the circus. Once with the man who would become my husband, I rode the carousel in the Tuilieries in Paris, in the middle of the night. Sure, I know that there is part of my behavior that is simply wish fulfillment. But I also think, at times, that I am the philosophical counterbalance to all those teenage girls, piling on so much makeup that they look like drag queens. Giving myself what I want, doing the things I never could as a kid, is the emotional equivalent of a "make-under." It's like washing off all that makeup and showing the world my true face.

Ever since my husband and I moved to Los Angeles, we have been making a tradition of Sunday suppers. We both like to cook, although we are of two different minds in the kitchen. Jason is all about precision. Never before had I ever bothered to make sure that the oven was preheated to the exact temperature, never before had I seen someone who when adjusting a recipe actually took out a paper and pen to figure out how to double six-eighths of a cup or what exactly half of two and three-quarters cups of whole milk is. Because of this, there are some dishes that Jason makes exquisitely. Growing up Panamanian, I was taught to cook in the Latin and Caribbean tradition of improvisation. "How much salt should I put in?" I would ask my mother when I helped make the arroz con pollo. "Just throw," she said. "And remember it is easier to add more but next to impossible to take too much out." My mother grocery shopped on Saturday and spent a good part of Sunday afternoon "seasoning" the meat and chicken for the week. If we had chicken on Thursday, it had been sitting in the fridge for three days, marinating in a bed of spices. I may not know how to measure well in the kitchen, but flavor is my specialty. The first time I saw my husband take a chicken breast out of its wrapping and throw it, dry, into a pan, I nearly wept.

Over the years, we have learned that while we make a good couple, we actually don't cook well together. Jason likes to prep each item, getting all the chopping and slicing and measuring done before he even turns on the stove. I like to blast my music, jazz or salsa or Jacques Brel, and flow with the music. It makes me crazy if Jason does not use enough spices. "The recipe doesn't call for those spices!" he says, as I assault him with packets of Sazón Goya. "That's because it's common sense!" I tell him. "There's no need to write it down." On the other hand, God forbid, the recipe calls for thinly sliced cucumber and I am slicing it thickly. The truth is that I don't really know what *julienne* means. If I wake up in the morning and I want the carrots to be diced, I do that. If I want them to be sliced, I do that. I think that if I'm going to eat it, then I can cut it however I please.

In the interest of not divorcing over a carrot, we take turns cooking our Sunday suppers. More often than not, Jason cooks the entées because he is a virtuoso and I am lazy. I am perfectly happy to pour the wine and make dessert. Grapefruit black pepper granita is my current specialty, but there's no shame in my game. I will serve up a silver bowl of Tofutti Cuties or a plate of slice-and-bake sugar cookies in a New York minute. When we make Sunday supper, we aren't trying to impress anyone. One night, when dinner for four swelled to dinner for twelve, we improvised. We got a rack of already cooked ribs from Trader Joes. Jason steamed dumplings from the Korean market; and I made a cucumber salad, tossed in a rice wine vinaigrette with black sesame seeds. We sautéed shrimp in olive oil and threw in halves of tiny baby potatoes. There was plenty of wine, and I made grapefruit granita for dessert. Nobody cared and nobody asked what we made from scratch and what we had bought from the store.

That said, there are times when I enjoy a culinary challenge. This past spring, my television agent, Alan, and his wife, Lora, were coming to dinner. We had also invited my friend Yahlin. Jason had been out playing soccer for most of the day, and we found ourselves, at two P.M., slightly panicked about what we were going to feed the guests who were arriving at five. Jason wanted to go with an old reliable—salmon or snapper or a roasted chicken. But I was tired of eating the same things, Sunday after Sunday. What I wanted to eat, what I had been longing for was lobster potpie. On an early date, we had driven out to Sag Harbor on Long Island in the fall, long after the summer crowds were gone. My favorite seafood shop was still open, and Jason and I had brought home several frozen lobster potpies. We heated the first one, casually, happy to have a prepared meal and hopeful that once unfrozen, the potpie would still taste good. We ate the second one several days later with all the voracious hunger of an addict on a binge. We rushed home from work, we locked the front door and we did not answer the phone. To me, a lobster potpie is the very embodiment of everything I love about summer: the beach, the sun, the stars, all baked into doughy perfection. It was Sunday in Los Angeles, and I was feeling homesick for the East Coast. I wanted to make lobster potpie.

Jason rolled his eyes. Lobster was expensive. We'd never made it before. He was tired from playing soccer. Couldn't I be more reasonable? I took out one of my favorite cookbooks, Ina Garten's *The Barefoot Contessa*. I made a quick assessment of the recipe and realized that the real impediment to lobster potpie is not the filling. The heavy lifting comes in making a pastry shell from scratch. So Jason and I made a deal. He would go to Costco and buy two pounds of fresh lobster meat. I would go to the grocery store for frozen pie shells and the remaining ingredients. And I would make the pie. If it came out miserably, we could always eat crow and order takeout. This is not false modesty. The first time I made a roast chicken, I undercooked it and found myself with a mouth full of pink, and slightly bloody, chicken breast. I was so disgusted that I couldn't just put it back in the oven and cook it some more. I had to throw it away. Just a few months ago, I was making a chicken dish for my husband. It was simple, a chicken breast, over a bed of spinach, topped with a mixture of chorizo and cannelini beans. The problem is I had the crazy idea to try to "marinate" the chicken in a mixture of sea salt and lemon juice. I thought it would be okay to just dust the sea salt off, I didn't realize that the chicken had absorbed it like a sponge. Every bite felt like we were chugging from a salt shaker. My husband, in an effort to be kind, ate two-thirds of it. Not me. Two bites and I was done. I screwed up. I don't have to eat the terrible thing to prove a point.

More often than not, though, I am a pretty good home cook. That's the thing about the joy of doing things badly—if practice doesn't always make perfect, it can make things pretty darn good. As I've mentioned before, one habit I've formed over the years is to double the most delicious ingredient in a recipe. I knew this was going to be critical if I was going to improvise a lobster potpie, just a few hours before our guests were due to arrive. Yes, I was going to cheat and use a frozen pie shell, but I wanted there to be plenty of lobster in every bite. Well, it turns out that I kind of overestimated the lobster. As the filling bubbled over, easy as pie—just lobster, yellow onion, fennel, butter, frozen peas, frozen onions and heavy cream—it became clear that I had enough lobster to feed a dozen hungry sailors. So I made not one, not two, but four lobster potpies. In an effort to jazz up my frozen shells, I melted a stick of butter and brushed the inside of each one. I filled one shell with lobster filling, then used another shell as the topping. It wasn't the prettiest pie. I did not have time to defrost them properly and the shell that went on top had to be pried from the tin. But the pies were delicious. And our guests loved them so much that I sent a pie home with my agent and his wife and half of a pie home with my friend. But more than that, it taught me the importance of not always cooking Sunday supper on automatic pilot. That night, I feasted not just on lobster but on the sweetness of memory.

My whole life has been a series of wishes—wishes to erase the pain of the past, wishes for a future I hope to create. The funny thing about Sunday supper is that it is a rit-

ual that has fulfilled wishes I never had the wherewithal
to articulate. Planning each meal is an exercise in creativ-
ity and an adventure for the senses—whether it's buying
flowers at the wholesale market downtown, or setting the
table with candles and our good china, or shopping for
vegetables at the Korean market. Sunday suppers require
teamwork—each time we cook a meal together, my husband and I discover new strengths and gifts. Sometimes, I
surprise him by taking over the heavy lifting. Always, he
amazes me with his ability to keep a cool head. Nine times
out of ten, in the hour before the guests arrive, we will
have a petty fight: about music or the meal or why we insist on throwing dinner parties as if we were Nick and
Nora in *The Thin Man.* Because we don't want to greet our
guests mad, these little tiffs force us to hone our making-
up skills: get it out and get over it. It's not fake, because
there is always a point in the meal, when our house is full
of friends and we are stuffed to the gills, when I look over
at him and know how lucky I am to have found him. And
the meals sustain us, long after our guests are gone and
the kitchen is cleaned. When we are bored and stuck in
traffic, at the airport, in a doctor's office, Jason will turn
to me and ask me to name the top ten meals that we cook
and the names of our Sunday suppers come tumbling out:
my quickie version of Julia's coq au vin, Jason's roast
chicken, island roast pork salad, Tahitian crabmeat soup,

Korean dumplings and BBQ ribs, our Spanish tapas supper, lobster potpie . . .

∞

VERONICA'S LAZY CONTESSA LOBSTER POTPIE

4 TO 5 SERVINGS

1½ cups chopped yellow onion (1 large onion)

¾ cup chopped fennel (1 fennel bulb)

1 stick unsalted butter

½ cup all-purpose flour

2½ cups fish stock or clam juice

1 tablespoon Pernod

1½ teaspoons kosher salt

¾ teaspoon freshly ground black pepper

3 tablespoons heavy cream

¾ pound cooked fresh lobster meat

1½ cups frozen peas (not baby peas)

1½ cups frozen small whole onions

½ cup minced flat-leaf parsley

2 frozen 9-inch pie crusts, thawed

egg wash (1 egg beaten with 2 tablespoons water)

Preheat the oven to 375°F.

Sauté the chopped onion and fennel in the butter in a large sauté pan over medium heat until the onions are translucent, 10 to 15 minutes. Add the flour and cook on low heat for 3 more minutes, stirring occasionally. Slowly add the stock, Pernod, salt, and pepper and simmer for 5 more minutes. Add the heavy cream.

Cut the lobster meat into medium-size cubes. Place the lobster, peas, whole onions, and parsley in a bowl (there is no need to defrost the vegetables). Pour the sauce over the mixture and check the seasonings. Set aside.

Fill one pie crust (already in tin) with the lobster mixture. Top with the second crust. Crimp the crusts together, and brush with the egg wash. Make 4 or 5 slashes in the top crust, and bake for 1 hour and 15 minutes, until the top is golden brown and the filling is bubbling hot.

About the Author

Veronica Chambers is the author of *When Did You Stop Loving Me* (aka *Miss Black America*), *Having It All?*, and *Mama's Girl*. She was formerly the culture writer for *Newsweek*, a senior associate editor at *Premiere*, and an executive editor at *Savoy*. Her writing has appeared in many magazines, including *Glamour*, *Vogue*, *Esquire*, the *New York Times Magazine*, and *O, The Oprah Magazine*. She lives in France with her husband.

Visit Veronica at VeronicaChambers.com. To receive her *Joy* newsletter, send an e-mail to joyofdoingthings badly@yahoo.com, with **I want some JOY!** in the subject line. For college lectures and *Joy* workshops, please contact Veronica's lecture agents at www.soapboxinc.com.

Sujean Rim is a freelance illustrator whose work can be seen every day on DailyCandy.com. In addition to illustrating, Sujean designs shoes. She lives in Brooklyn.